Paths of our Children

HISTORIC INDIANS OF ARKANSAS

by George Sabo III

Arkansas Archeological Survey
Popular Series No. 3

©1992
Arkansas Archeological Survey
and Arkansas Humanities Council
Revised Edition ©2001
Reprinted 2009

Library of Congress Cataloging-in-Publication Data

Sabo, George.
  Paths of our children : historic Indians of Arkansas / by George Sabo
III.-- Rev. ed.
      p. cm. -- (Arkansas Archeological Survey popular series ; no. 3)

Includes bibliographical references and index.
  ISBN 1-56349-092-7
  1. Indians of North America--Arkansas--History. I. Title. II. Popular
series (Arkansas Archeological Survey) ; no. 3.
  E78.A8 S23 2001
  976.7'00497--dc21
                                2001003260

Cover Art: "Sequoyah" by Charles Banks Wilson
Printed by: PMC Solutions, University of Arkansas

The original publication was supported in part through a grant from the
Arkansas Humanities Council and the
National Endowment for the Humanities.
The Arkansas Archeological Survey is a unit of the
University of Arkansas System.

Contents

Preface

When French explorers entered the central Mississippi Valley late in the seventeenth century, they encountered Indians who called themselves the O-gah-pah, or Downstream People. The native guides who led the Frenchmen used the term Arkansas to identify these Indians. The latter term stuck and became the name of the territory and then the state that Euroamericans created. The contemporary descendants of seventeenth century Arkansas Indians are known as Quapaws. Other Indians whose lands became part of Arkansas include the Caddos, Tunicas, Koroas, and Osages. During the eighteenth and nineteenth centuries, these tribes were joined by Cherokees and others who were displaced from homelands east of the Mississippi. Most of the tribes remaining in Arkansas at the turn of the nineteenth century were ultimately removed to Indian Territory in Kansas, Oklahoma, and Texas. Despite the calamitous effects of environmental changes, disease, removal, and government oppression these groups found ways to adapt to ever-changing circumstances. They were able to endure and keep alive cherished values and beliefs. With the exception of the Koroas, who joined the Natchez in the eighteenth century, each of these groups today maintains a distinctive cultural identity.

This book provides a brief introduction to the historic Indians of Arkansas. It was written to accompany *Crossroads of the Past: 12,000 Years of Indian Life in Arkansas* by Frank Schambach and Leslie Newell, which deals mainly with the prehistoric Indians of Arkansas.

I begin in Chapter 1 with a brief review of this prehistory. Chapter 2 provides information gleaned from the accounts of Hernando de Soto's expedition, which spent most of the years 1542 and 1543 wandering through Arkansas. Even though it is difficult to verify the cultural identities of many of the Indians mentioned in the De Soto accounts, these chronicles provide interesting and valuable clues about what life was like in sixteenth century Arkansas. Information from accounts written by seventeenth and eighteenth century Europeans is used in Chapter 3 to provide sketches of the Indians living in Arkansas when the activities of French and Spanish explorers, traders, and missionaries began to open up the region for European settlement. These sketches are followed by a brief review in Chapter 4 of some of the more significant events that affected the lives of Indian people during the nineteenth and twentieth centuries. An attempt is made to provide a balanced perspective on Indian experiences during the historic era by incorporating information on the Indians' own responses to the events that most profoundly affected their traditional ways. The group- by-group organization of these two chapters results in a bit of repetition and masks some of the intergroup dynamics that characterized these periods, but many interested readers—including educators and the contemporary descendents of the groups described here—find this format more useful for their purposes. A brief summary of the current status of these groups is presented in Chapter 5.

I am grateful to a number of colleagues whose assistance led to significant improvements in the content and organization of this book. Frank F. Schambach and Hester A. Davis both reviewed several versions of the draft with painstaking care; other reviewers include Ann Early, Charles Ewen, Michael Hoffman, Martha Rolingson, and Carrie Wilson. The wisdom shared by numerous Caddos, Cherokees, Quapaws, Osages, and Tunicas during many events to which they have welcomed me immeasurably benefited my efforts. Elaine Reynolds organized the original set of pictorial illustrations that grace these pages. Deborah Sabo and Mary Lynn Kennedy were responsible for final editing and manuscript layout of this revised edition. I sincerely appreciate these donations of talent and expertise. Whatever shortcomings remain in this work are my own responsibility.

Editor's Note to the 2009 Reprint. We have taken this opportunity to correct a few minor typographical errors. In addition, we have corrected the photo attribution in the figure caption on page 83, and removed a statement from page 86 that contained erroneous details about a trading post at Spadra Bluff.

1

ANCIENTS:
Arkansas Prehistory

The Paleoindian Era

Many thousands of years ago, before any people arrived, the lands that later became Arkansas were very different than they are today. The climate was cool and moist. Much of the region was covered with coniferous forests and grasslands. Mammoths, mastodons, and other Ice Age animals roamed the land. There were few edible plants, and the rivers were too cold and swift for most aquatic species.

Around 9500 years ago, small groups of Native American hunters began to arrive, whom archeologists call Paleoindians. Descending the Mississippi Valley from the northern Great Plains, a few of these groups, with only 25 to 50 members each, remained in the Delta lands of eastern Arkansas where a deciduous bottom-land forest harbored abundant useful resources. Adapted to Ice Age conditions with a well-designed Stone Age technology, their descendants expanded into the Ozark and Ouachita Mountains and the Gulf Coastal Plain.

Keys to Paleoindian success were their skill in using available resources, their ability to relay information about those resources to neighbors in adjacent areas, and their cleverness in revising strategies when environments changed. Chert, for example, an important resource from the mountainous parts of Arkansas, was acquired and used by Paleoindians across the entire state to make tools and weapons. And, as extinction removed Ice Age animals from the landscape, hunting technologies and techniques changed accordingly. Deer, elk, and other species were targeted instead as the preferred sources of meat, hides, antlers, and other animal products.

Paleoindian success in adapting to regional conditions permitted their populations to increase. By 8500 B.C. Paleoindians were making a new kind of tool, which archeologists call the Dalton point. These points have been found across Arkansas and the Mid-South, indicating the spread of Paleoindian groups. Dalton points were an important part of the throwing stick and dart complex used for hunting game animals. Some of these points were also used as butchering implements, and many broken specimens were reworked for continued service as scrapers, drills, and other tools. The Dalton people began to manufacture stone-bladed adzes for woodworking tasks as deciduous forests expanded with warming climates. The Sloan site in northeast Arkansas is a Dalton cemetery, attesting to beliefs in an afterlife and associated burial practices.

The Archaic Era

Drought conditions affecting many upland areas drove some groups into the major river valleys after 7900 B.C., where populations continued to thrive. Small settled communities developed and an increasing variety of natural resources were used, including nuts, fish, deer, raccoon, opossum, turkey, shellfish, fruits, and berries. Forest cutting and soil disturbance around Indian settlements created habitats by 4500 B.C. that attracted a variety of weeds and grasses with nutritious seeds. The use of these plants as food, along with attempts to manage their growth, led to the development of cultivation techniques by 2000 B.C. Plant species domesticated in this way included lambsquarters, knotweed, sumpweed, sunflower, maygrass, little barley, and several varieties of squashes.

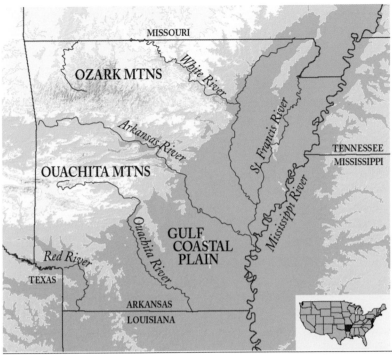

Physiography and boundary of the present-day state of Arkansas

Indians of the Poverty Point culture (2000–500 B.C.) built the first town and monumental earthworks in North America near present-day Epps, Louisiana. Extensive trade networks brought exotic materials from across eastern North America to Poverty Point sites located throughout the lower Mississippi Valley. Artifacts such as finely crafted stone "locust effigy" beads found on sites in Arkansas reveal participation in this exchange network. The decline of Poverty Point culture around 500 B.C. remains a mystery.

Increasing dietary reliance on plant foods including nuts and seeds led to the development of new techniques for manufacturing waterproof fired-clay pottery containers by 600 B.C. Used at first for boiling acorns to remove tannic acid, and later for cooking dried grains, pottery technology revolutionized Native American food storage and preparation methods.

The Woodland Era

The Hopewell culture of Ohio and Illinois flourished between 500 B.C. and A.D. 500 and influenced populations across eastern North America. Trade in exotic goods and elaborate burials for community leaders were two hallmarks of this culture. A Hopewell-style log tomb was discovered beneath a burial mound near Helena, Arkansas. The logs were oak, some measuring nearly four feet in diameter. The honored dead were buried with copper-covered panpipes, conch shell drinking cups from the Gulf of Mexico, and necklaces and bracelets made of shell beads and wolf teeth.

Native Americans in the Mississippi Valley began to use the bow and arrow towards the end of the Hopewell era. This was such an efficient weapon that by A.D. 500 it had largely replaced the throwing stick and dart. Tribal warfare witnessed by early European explorers seems to have begun about the time the bow and arrow appeared.

The development of gardening, pottery technology, and more effective hunting weapons stimulated population growth and led to the emergence of settled village life after A.D. 500. Corn, originally domesticated in Mexico, was adopted by many groups in the Mississippi Valley between A.D. 900 and 1200. The shift to grain-based diets gave rise to a preference for adding salt to prepared food. The production of salt for trade became an important activity in southwest Arkansas, where there are many natural salt springs.

Among the first to build large platform mounds in the Southeast were the Plum Bayou Indians. Beginning around A.D. 750, they built the site now preserved as Toltec Mounds State Park near Scott, Arkansas. Here, 18 dome- and platform-shaped mounds, two of which today stand 41 and 49 feet high, were surrounded by a 5298-foot-long, 6-foot-high embankment with a ditch on its outer side. Several of the mounds are aligned with solstice and equinox sunrise and sunset positions. The Plum Bayou Indians hunted with bows and arrows and raised maygrass, little barley, lambsquarters, squash, and corn in their gardens.

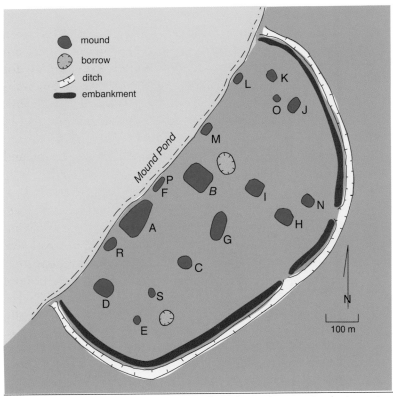

The Toltec site reconstructed from historic and archeological study

The Mississippi Era

In the centuries after A.D. 900, Indians across the Southeast turned from hunting, gathering, and gardening to a way of life based on agricultural production of corn, beans, and squash. These communities grew rapidly. In many localities, large fortified towns were built, some with platform mounds used for ceremonial purposes. These Mississippian societies were highly organized with powerful leaders, productive agricultural economies, and long-distance trade networks.

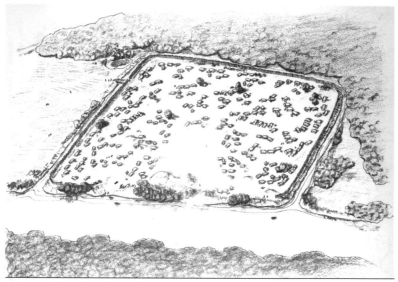

"The Parkin site" by Linda Murphy

One example of a large, well-organized Mississippian society is the Parkin culture, represented by several archeological sites in eastern Arkansas. The key site, preserved as Parkin Archeological State Park, was a fortified village containing a large earthen mound and dozens of houses. This site was occupied up to the sixteenth century, when Spanish explorers led by Hernando de Soto became the first Europeans to meet the native people of the interior Southeast. In fact, archeologists believe that the Parkin site is the town of Casqui, which was visited by De Soto's army in the summer of 1541.

The accounts left by members of De Soto's expedition brought the prehistoric era to a close and marked the beginning of the historic era, when written records became an increasingly important source of information on Native American and European encounters. We will examine that era next.

2

ANCESTORS:
The Sixteenth Century

Early Spanish Exploration in the Southeast

In the years following the voyages of Christopher Columbus, Spaniards living on the island of Hispaniola (now Haiti and the Dominican Republic) discovered the mainland of North America. At least three vessels surveyed the southeastern coastlines between 1513 and 1519.

These voyages were followed by a series of land expeditions to explore the continent (which they called La Florida), looking for populations to enslave and for new sources of wealth. Each of these ventures ended in failure. In 1521 Juan Pónce de León lost his life in an unsuccessful attempt to establish a settlement along the Atlantic coast of the Florida peninsula.

In 1526 Lucas Vásquez de Ayllón put ashore with about 600 settlers somewhere along the coast of present-day Georgia or South Carolina, to found a colony named San Miguel de Gualdape. After only three months Ayllón was dead, his colony abandoned.

In 1528, Pánfilo de Narváez landed on the western coast of the Florida peninsula with around 400 soldiers and about 40 horses, planning to strike inland, discover unknown native civilizations, and claim whatever prizes he could find. Eight years later, four survivors

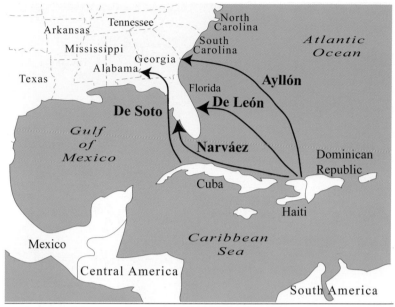

Early Spanish voyages to the North American southeast

of this expedition were rescued in northern Mexico, having traveled on foot from the Texas coast. These early failures of European attempts to gain a foothold in North America suggest that the course of later history might have been quite different had the Indians escaped decimation from Old World diseases that were introduced by these expeditions.

Undaunted by these earlier failures and with confidence built upon his participation in highly successful conquests in Mexico and Peru, Hernando de Soto, in 1539, landed in Tampa Bay on the west coast of Florida with a force of between 600 and 700 men (most of whom were soldiers and military officers; there were also a few craftsmen, priests, and two women), about 225 horses, and an assortment of war dogs and pigs. Thus began the most protracted Spanish war of conquest ever undertaken in southeastern North America. De Soto's expedition lasted four years. After trekking up the Florida peninsula and traversing territories that would become Georgia, North

"Spanish Hulk," by Gary Simmons (courtesy of the artist)

and South Carolina, Tennessee, Alabama, and Mississippi, he brought the first Europeans ever to cross the Mississippi River.

A considerable amount of research has been undertaken to determine the route followed by De Soto's expedition through southeastern North America, beginning with the early eighteenth century studies of the French map maker Guillaume Delisle and continuing to the present. These efforts have been universally plagued by characteristics of sixteenth century exploration accounts that make it difficult to reconstruct travel routes and details of events that took place during the expeditions. Information concerning De Soto's expedition varies greatly among the available accounts, owing to differences in the purposes for which each account was written and differences in the perspectives, biases, and observational abilities of the various authors. Furthermore, most of these accounts are available today only in the form of later printed editions, the original manuscripts having been lost. This makes it difficult to identify changes, whether accidental or intentional, made in the reprinted accounts and in the various translations.

Only three first-hand accounts of De Soto's expedition are known to exist, although a summary of another previously unknown account has been discovered recently. These were written by Luys Hernandez de Biedma (the representative of King Charles V), Rodrigo Ranjel (De Soto's secretary), and an anonymous Portuguese gentleman from the town of Elvas. Biedma's account—the only one that survives to the present in original manuscript form—is very brief, while those of Ranjel and Elvas provide much more detail. Unfortunately, substantial differences in the sequence of events described and in the quality of information characterize these latter two accounts. Ranjel's, which provides a valuable daily itinerary of the expedition, is preserved only in Volume IV of Gonzalo Fernández de Oviedo's *Historia general y natural de las Indias*, published in 1851. Oviedo abbreviated Ranjel's diary, added some commentary of his own, and apparently omitted all chapters on the final year of the expedition.

A much-used account by Garcilaso de la Vega (who did not participate in the expedition) was written about 40 years after the fact but it incorporates much information obtained from interviews with at least three of the expedition's survivors. Since the information given in these accounts is very uneven, scholars attempting to use only these sources to reconstruct De Soto's route are forced either to rely mainly on a single account or to pick and choose from the information provided in all accounts, neither of which is a satisfactory approach.

The first thorough attempt in the modern era to reconstruct De Soto's route was commissioned by Congress in 1936 to commemorate the 400th anniversary of the army's landing in Florida. The report, written by John R. Swanton of the Smithsonian Institution and published in 1939, made use of the Biedma, Elvas, Garcilaso, and Rangel accounts. Swanton incorporated geographical information on the regions the army was believed to have traversed, as well as what little archeological information was then available. Swanton's reconstruction was far more convincing than preceding ones and consequently it gained quick and widespread acceptance. Most discussions of De Soto's route found in modern history textbooks are based on the findings of the Swanton report.

During the past decade, Dr. Charles Hudson of the University of Georgia has reexamined the De Soto accounts and compared them with new translations of accounts written by other Spanish explorers who retraced parts of De Soto's route. Hudson also considered modern archeological data on the distribution of sixteenth century Indian populations across southeastern North America. These newly available sources led Hudson to propose a route that differs substantially from the one reconstructed by Swanton. Hudson's version of De Soto's route stimulated considerable debate among scholars and inspired a renewed effort on the part of archeologists to examine more closely the evidence of sixteenth century contact between Spanish explorers and American Indians.

Hudson's version of De Soto's route differs most extensively from Swanton's reconstruction in the portions west of the Mississippi River. According to Hudson, De Soto and his army spent the better part of two years during 1541–1543 (out of four years total)

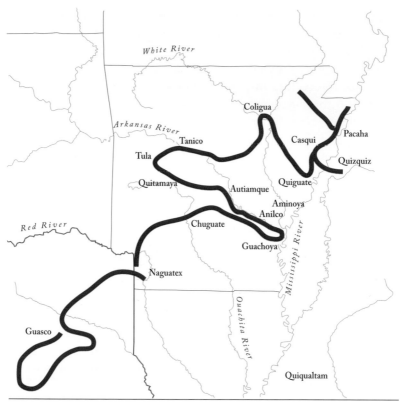

Hudson's reconstruction of Hernando De Soto's route through Arkansas and Texas

wandering through Arkansas. (In contrast, Swanton's reconstruction had De Soto's army passing through the state in less than a year, June 1541 to March 1542.) The Hudson reconstruction naturally attracted much interest on the part of Arkansas scholars. A thorough assessment of archeological data on sixteenth century Indian population distributions in Arkansas conducted by Dr. Dan Morse, Dr. Ann Early, and Dr. Frank Schambach of the Arkansas Archeological Survey led to subsequent modifications and refinements of Hudson's version of the route. The discussion below of De Soto's encounters with the Indians in Arkansas is based on this reconstruction.

"De Soto Discovering the Mississippi River," from the 1902 supplement to the St. Louis Globe-Democrat (courtesy of the Missouri Historical Society, OSL319)

The Spaniards Enter Arkansas

By the spring of 1541, when they reached the Mississippi River, the Spaniards had spent two years traversing the Southeast. They encountered numerous Indian villages, from which they supplied themselves with food, and they enslaved hundreds, if not thousands, to serve as bearers and concubines. They found no precious metals or jewels, but in their battles with Indians the Spaniards lost many men and horses. Nonetheless, the army remained sufficiently large to appear awesome and formidable to native peoples who never before had seen Europeans, horses, or armored war dogs.

On 8 May 1541 (in the Old Style or Julian calendar) De Soto's army entered the Indian province of Quizquiz, which modern scholars believe was on the eastern side of the Mississippi River, in present-day Mississippi and Tennessee. Here the Spaniards were visited by Aquixo, a prominent Indian leader from a province on the opposite side of the great river. In sixteenth century Spanish accounts, the leader of a native community was called a cacique (pronounced ka-see'-kay). Often the leader's name was used to refer not only to his or her person, but also to the main village in which he or she resided, and the province or district over which he or she ruled.

Aquixo claimed that both his province and Quizquiz were subject to a more powerful leader named Pacaha, who lived farther north on the west side of the Mississippi River. Spurred by the hope that after two long years they might finally have come upon a wealthy Indian population, the Spaniards spent four weeks constructing four large rafts. On the morning of 18 June they crossed to the western bank of the Mississippi.

De Soto passed through the now-abandoned province of Aquixo and turned north. After two days of very difficult travel, he entered the province of Casqui, located in a verdant part of the central Mississippi Valley one chronicler described as being "well peopled with large towns, two or three of which could be seen from one town," with fields of corn and groves of nut and fruit trees in the open spaces between the towns. On 24 June the Spaniards reached the main town of Casqui and remarked that these Indians lived in "very good cabins." Modern scholars believe this town is the Parkin site (now Parkin Archeological State Park) in Cross County. Several sixteenth century brass hawk's bells, a faceted glass bead, and lead shot have been found at Parkin. (The bells are a type known as "Clarksdale" bells named after a sixteenth century site in Clarksdale, Mississippi, where a number of them were found.)

The Spaniards were met by the leader of Casqui, who presented gifts to De Soto and offered to provide lodging for his army. According to the accounts, a severe drought was destroying the Indians' crops, and De Soto's help in bringing rain was requested. De Soto ordered his men to erect a wooden cross on the summit of a large earthen mound in the center of the village, and a ceremony of adoration was performed. The next day it rained, convincing the Indians—so say the accounts—of De Soto's claim that he was the "son of the sun."

"Ceremonial Cross Raising at Parkin," by Dan Kerlin (courtesy of the University of Arkansas Museum)

From Casqui the Spaniards pushed on to Pacaha, where De Soto was led to believe there might be gold. Though no gold was found, the Spaniards were impressed by what they saw when they reached the main town. Rodrigo Ranjel described the town as "a very good one, thoroughly well stockaded; walls were furnished with towers and a ditch round about, for the most part full of water which flows in by a canal from the river." Archeologists now believe that the capital of Pacaha was located along Bradley Ridge in Crittenden County.

The Spaniards also learned of a long-standing rivalry between Casqui and Pacaha. During a quarrel between the two leaders, Pacaha is reported to have told Casqui, "you know well that I am a greater lord than you, and of more honorable parents and grandparents, and that to me belongs a higher place." To this Casqui replied, "True it is that you are a greater lord than I, and that your forebears were greater than mine. But you know that I am older and mightier than you, and that I confine you in your walls whenever I wish, and you have never seen my country." If the Spanish chroniclers succeeded in capturing even a general sense of the argument between Casqui and

Pacaha, then it appears that the leaders of these two rival provinces both laid claim to their chiefly status by virtue of their birthright, not unlike the claims to office made by European monarchs of the time. It also appears that individual strengths and abilities tempered these claims—another political reality that would not have been foreign to the Europeans, whose own history was punctuated by contentious and often bloody struggles between rival "heirs" to the throne.

De Soto remained at Pacaha for more than a month, sending small groups of soldiers out to explore the countryside. One group traveled to the northwest and reached the province of Caluc, where they encountered roving Indians who were hunting and fishing and living in shelters consisting of a wooden framework covered by sewn rush mats. Archeologists believe that Caluc was located beyond the lowlands west of Crowley's Ridge—perhaps along the Black River and its tributaries—and that these people were actually members of a sedentary agricultural society engaged in summer hunting and fishing expeditions.

From Pacaha the Spaniards returned briefly to Casqui, then continued southward along the St. Francis River to the main village of another province, called Quiguate. The Spaniards described Quiguate as the largest town they had visited.

At Quiguate, De Soto learned about another province named Coligua, located in mountainous lands to the northwest. Since the Spaniards believed that gold or silver would most likely be found in mountainous regions, they spent a week slogging through swampy, uninhabited terrain to reach the "River of Coligua" (the White River) along the eastern edge of the Ozark Mountains. The Indians of this province (located in the vicinity of Batesville) were surprised by the Spaniards' sudden approach, indicating there was no communication with Indians living farther south who had already met De Soto. The Spaniards found many buffalo hides at Coligua, but no gold.

To feed themselves, the Spaniards confiscated food—mainly corn and beans—from the Indians. The route of travel was determined in part, therefore, by the locations of major towns in native agricultural regions, where the Indians—called Mississippians by modern archeologists—kept central storehouses filled with large quantities of corn and other foods. With food supplies short at Coligua and reckoning that prospects would be unfavorable were they to continue north, the Spaniards turned southwest.

Over the next few days the Spaniards passed through several provinces. At Calpista they found "an excellent salt spring." The Spaniards were in such desperate need of salt that many had died from a lack of it by this point in the expedition. This must have been in the vicinity of the confluence of Departee Creek and the White River in northern White County, where a Confederate salt works was later built at the only salt source known in the region. At Palisema, along the Little Red River, the Spaniards found a few scattered houses and only a little corn. At Tutilcoya, probably near Conway, De Soto learned about a large province located farther up the "River of Cayas," which we now believe was the Arkansas River. On 16 September, the Spaniards arrived at the settlement of Tanico in the province of Cayas. Cayas was a well-populated region with many fields of corn, but here the Indians were living in scattered settlements quite different from the compact fortified towns found along the Mississippi and St. Francis rivers. The Spaniards remained in Cayas for three weeks. They saw Indians making salt at brackish ponds by straining the brine through baskets and boiling it. The Indians of Cayas evidently carried some of this salt to other provinces where it was traded for other goods.

From Tanico the Spaniards crossed the Arkansas River and traveled upstream to another mountainous area where they entered the province of Tula. The Tula Indians spoke a language that guides from Tanico could not understand. Modern scholars believe these were a Caddoan-speaking people located in the northern Ouachita Mountains in the vicinity of Fort Smith. The expedition accounts mention that the Tula were buffalo hunters. Being used to hunting large game, the Tula were not intimidated, as other Indians had been, by the Spanish cavalry. When the Caddo attacked, the Tula used long wooden lances to kill several horses and men.

Finding no gold in the mountains and little food at Tula, the Spaniards turned back toward the central Mississippi Valley, passing through the provinces of Quipana and Quitamaya, the latter located in the vicinity of Benton. Continuing east, the Spaniards came again to the Arkansas River about midway between Little Rock and Pine Bluff. Here they spent the winter of 1541–1542 (December to early March) at the main town of the province of Autiamque.

Their relationship with the Indians had steadily deteriorated during the preceding months, so the Spaniards considered it necessary to erect a stockade around the part of the town they occupied. Though abundant food supplies were available at Autiamque, it was so cold that the Spaniards would oftentimes venture out of the village only long enough to gather firewood. For an entire month they were snow-bound. Juan Ortiz, a survivor from the Narvàez expedition (an earlier Spanish expedition that set ashore in Florida in 1528) whom De Soto had rescued and who thereafter had served as a translator, died that winter. From that point on, the Spaniards had considerable difficulty communicating with the Indians.

In the spring of 1542 De Soto led his dwindling army farther down the Arkansas River through the province of Ayays to Anilco. Archeologists believe that Anilco was located at or near the Menard-Hodges site, on the southern tip of Little Prairie north of the Arkansas River in southern Arkansas County. Here the Spaniards found another densely populated agricultural region described as the richest they had seen. According to one account, the Indians had abandoned the main town prior to the arrival of the Spaniards and set fire to the house of the cacique. Finding the food stores intact, the Spaniards occupied the town, but the Indians would steal back at night to carry off as much corn as they could. This put the Spaniards in increasingly desperate straits, since an enormous amount of food was required to feed the army and its many animals.

De Soto decided to move to Guachoya, a town located nearby on the south side of the Arkansas River just upstream from its confluence with the Mississippi. From there he hoped to find out how far it was to the sea. If a settlement with enough food could be found, he planned to move his army there and construct boats to send to Cuba for much needed supplies. At Guachoya the Spaniards found a well-stockaded town, but the Indians had left, taking their food with them.

De Soto therefore decided to send out a cavalry detachment to explore the area farther south, hoping that another town with food, or else a route to the sea, would be found. The detachment returned eight days later, reporting that they had traveled only 14 or 15 leagues (a league being approximately 3 miles distance) through boggy and desolate country. Disheartened by this news, alarmed by the increasing boldness of the Indians, and growing more and more doubtful about his prospects for success, De Soto sent a message to another cacique named Quigualtam, a powerful leader whose province was said to be some distance farther down the Mississippi River. De Soto claimed again he was the "son of the sun" and demanded that "in token of love and obedience [Quigualtam] should bring him something of what was most esteemed in [his] land." Quigualtam replied that it was not his custom to visit anyone, that others served and obeyed him, and in reply to De Soto's claim to being the son of the sun, he said, "let him dry up the great river and he [Quigualtam] would believe him."

Quigualtam's reply enraged De Soto, now feverishly ill. Fearing an Indian attack was imminent, the Spaniards attacked Anilco with such cruelty that even their own accounts of the battle reflect a distinct sense of remorse. The Spaniards gained little from their attack. On 21 May 1542 De Soto died, joining ranks with Pònce de León, Ayllón, and Narváez, all of whom lost their lives in the vain hope that wealth and glory would be found somewhere in this land.

Luis Moscoso de Alvarado succeeded De Soto as commander of the expedition. De Soto was quietly buried at Guachoya. The Spaniards attempted to keep his death a secret from the Indians, but the Indians noticed the grave and suspected De Soto's fate. The Spaniards, fearing knowledge of De Soto's death might bring an attack from the Indians, exhumed the corpse at night, wrapped it in blankets weighted with sand, and sank it in the Mississippi River. When the leader of Guachoya asked about De Soto, Moscoso replied that he had gone to the sky, as he had often done before.

Moscoso and the remaining soldiers (there were now about 300) decided that their best option at this point was to head toward Spanish settlements in Mexico. Two routes lay before them: down the Mississippi and along the Gulf Coast, or overland. The latter route was chosen with the hope that food would be available at Indian villages along the way. On 5 June the Spaniards departed from Guachoya.

Traveling up the Arkansas River, perhaps as far as Pine Bluff, the army headed west along the southern edge of the Ouachitas. The Spaniards passed through the province of Chuguate, along the Ouachita River between Malvern and Arkadelphia, where they observed Caddo Indians making salt. At Aguacay, along the Little Missouri River near Nashville, the Spaniards learned that they would have to travel farther to the southwest—to the Red River Valley—in order to find large populations with abundant food supplies.

Reaching the Red River Valley, the Spaniards entered the province of Naguatex, described as a very extensive settlement. Unlike the Mississippians, the Caddo Indians of this region had a settlement pattern consisting of small, scattered farmsteads, each with its own houses and fields, dispersed around local ceremonial centers near which community leaders and priests resided.

Here the Indians launched a well-organized attack that divided the Spanish forces and nearly succeeded in overwhelming them. An Indian captured by the Spaniards revealed that the attack had been a joint effort planned by the caciques of Naguatex, Amaye, and Hacanac. This Indian's further statement that the cacique of Naguatex was the "captain and head of all" indicates the existence of a large and well-organized chiefdom—much like Pacaha's—in which several towns, each with its own leader, were subject to a single very powerful leader.

To reach the main settlement area in the vicinity of Garland, the Spaniards had to cross the Red River, which they did only with much difficulty. They remained in Naguatex for a month. While they rested in the main town, Moscoso made it known that he wished to meet the cacique. Two days later messengers returned bearing the news that the cacique was on his way. The venerable chief soon

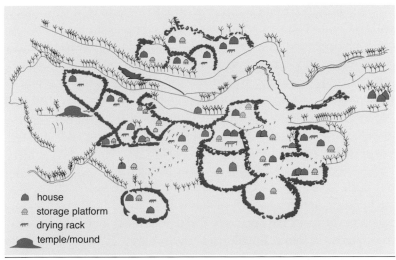

🛖	house
⌂	storage platform
🦗	drying rack
🗻	temple/mound

A schematic illustration of the 1690–91 Terán drawing of a historic Caddoan settlement along the Great Bend of the Red River (original in Archivo General de Indias, Seville)

arrived, "well attended by his men." According to one account, the Indians approached the Spaniards "one ahead of the other in double file, leaving a lane in the middle through which the cacique came." Moscoso treated the cacique well because he knew he would need this leader's help to continue the journey.

Upon leaving Naguatex, the Spaniards entered into present-day Texas, where they had trouble finding enough food for themselves and for their horses in the Indian villages they visited. The Spaniards were used to plundering Mississippian villages where produce from the surrounding countryside was stored near the residences of the leaders for later redistribution. The Caddo Indians did not practice this form of economic organization. Instead, harvested crops were stored in small, elevated granaries at the individual farmsteads, and each family contributed a share of their produce for the support of their leaders. To make matters worse for the Spaniards, these Indians also began to hide their corn.

Eventually, the expedition reached the province of Guasco, still in Caddo country, where the Indians possessed turquoise and cloth obtained in trade from tribes farther to the west. Here the Spaniards found some corn, and also learned of a "River of Daycoa" located 10 days travel toward the west, where a different group of Indians lived. Moscoso sent a detachment of men on the strongest horses to investigate. The soldiers found the area occupied by small groups of hunters and gatherers who spoke a language that the Guasco Indians could not understand.

This was the end of the trail for the Spaniards. They decided to return to the Mississippi River and spend the approaching winter building boats in which to descend to the gulf. The return trip was very difficult. Passing back through lands they had plundered, the Spaniards found hostile Indians and very little food. Only in the province of Naguatex had the Indians been able to refill their granaries with corn.

Returning to Anilco, the Spaniards found the Indians destitute. Following the destruction of their town by De Soto's men, they had neglected to plant their fields. Moscoso learned, however, of a rival province called Aminoya, located only two days travel to the north. There the Spaniards spent the winter, during which seven boats were constructed. In one of the few strokes of good luck the Spaniards experienced, the Mississippi River flooded shortly after the boats were completed in June 1543, and its waters reached to where the boats lay. On 2 July, the boats were eased into the water and the Spaniards, now numbering between 200 and 300, began their long voyage down the river. As they passed by Quigualtam's province, a hundred large war canoes were sent out to hurry the Spaniards along. When the Spaniards finally reached the mouth of the Mississippi River, a lone Indian standing on the bank called out: "If we possessed such large canoes as yours, we would follow you to your own land and conquer it, for we too are men like yourselves."

Cultural Identity of Sixteenth Century Indians

Who were the Indians the Spaniards encountered in Arkansas in the sixteenth century? This is a difficult question to answer

"Conquistadors" by Gary Simmons (courtesy of the artist)

for several reasons. The Spanish chroniclers typically provide only sketchy and often imprecise information about the Indians. The names attributed to groups the Spaniards met, or sometimes only heard about, may be names used by the people themselves, or names they were called by native guides or interpreters who spoke other languages. It is sometimes impossible to decide which is the case. Spanish chronicles often use the same name to identify a "province," its main town, and its leader. Does this mean that the leader assumed the name of the province when he came into power, or did the province take the name of its current leader? Finally, Spanish chroniclers undoubtedly introduced many phonetic errors when they transliterated Indian words to write them down. All these factors complicate our efforts to use exploration accounts to determine the cultural identity of sixteenth century native populations.

The most frustrating problem lies in the fact that the next group of Europeans to visit Arkansas—the French explorers Marquette and Jolliet, who came down the Mississippi River in 1673—used completely different names to identify the Indians they met. In the 130 years that transpired between the time of De Soto's visit and that of the French, the distribution of native populations across southeastern North America underwent tremendous change. For example, Marquette and Jolliet mention only a single Mitchigamea (an Illinoian Indian group) village in northeast Arkansas, a region De Soto had described as one of the most populous in all of southeastern North America. (Note, however, that Marquette and Jolliet did not explore interior regions adjacent to the Mississippi River. Conclusions about sixteenth century population declines based only on their accounts may not be warranted.)

The Indians identified by seventeenth century Frenchmen sometimes were groups that had been dislocated from former homelands. Others represented newly organized societies—that is, communities that had only recently developed from the coalesced remnants of previous groups shattered under the impacts of earlier Spanish invasions. Whether any of the groups identified in seventeenth century French accounts were descended from groups mentioned in sixteenth century Spanish accounts is a problem no one has solved.

On the basis of certain kinds of information provided in the De Soto accounts, however, some speculations can be made concerning possible cultural identities of native populations in sixteenth century Arkansas. First, linguistic boundaries separating Cayas and Tula, and

Anilco and Guachoya, can be identified. There certainly must have been other linguistic boundaries, but even this limited information is useful for identifying major linguistic groups. Southeastern North America is a region where extensive linguistic diversity existed among the native tribes. Anthropologists have found it useful to identify relationships between individual groups on the basis of their membership in broad "families" of closely related languages. The five major language families represented in the Southeast are Algonkian, Muskogean, Iroquoian, Siouan, and Caddoan.

Second, reports of instances in which Indians were "surprised" at the arrival of the Spaniards suggest a lack of communication between areas, which also may be interpreted as representing major cultural boundaries. Such a boundary evidently existed between the Casqui-Pacaha area, in northeastern Arkansas, and the province of Coligua, along the eastern fringes of the Ozarks. Biedma's statement that Spaniards arrived at Tula "before the inhabitants had any notice of us" also corresponds with the above-mentioned linguistic boundary separating that group from the inhabitants of the Arkansas River Valley.

A third category of helpful information consists of observations of native settlement patterns. The compact fortified towns identified for native provinces located along the Mississippi, St. Francis, and lower Arkansas rivers can be contrasted with the dispersed farmsteads observed in the province of Cayas farther up the Arkansas River and in the Caddo region of southwest Arkansas and eastern Texas.

Putting this information together, it is possible to speculate that sixteenth century cultural and linguistic boundaries defined the following regions: (1) the central Mississippi Valley region from Pacaha on the north to Anilco on the south, and extending up the Arkansas River as far as Autiamque; (2) the lower Mississippi Valley region extending from Guachoya to the south for an undetermined distance, but probably at least as far as Quigualtam; (3) the lower White River Valley region beginning at Coligua and extending for an undetermined distance up that valley; (4) a Ouachita Mountain region minimally including the Tula, whom we assume were

Caddoan speakers; and (5) a Red River Valley region of Caddoan speakers. It is possible, of course, that additional cultural boundaries may have existed.

Attributing modern tribal names to these five regions is a more difficult task. Least contentious is the suggested Caddoan identity of the sixteenth century inhabitants of the Red River Valley. This designation has considerable archeological and ethnohistoric support. Many scholars have suggested that the Tula Indians were a northern offshoot of the Caddo tribes living farther to the south, and some have suggested that they were antecedents of the Cahinnio Indians encountered in the Ouachita Mountain region by French explorers in the seventeenth and eighteenth centuries. Others have suggested that the Tula Indians were an ancestral group of Wichita Indians, another Caddoan-speaking group whose later historic settlements were located on the Southern Plains.

The cultural identities of the remaining groups have proved harder to determine and attempts to make such identifications stimulate considerable debate. A number of scholars suggest a Tunican affiliation for the groups along the Arkansas River in the province of Cayas and especially in the town of Tanico. Sixteenth century artifacts, including a brass hawk's bell of the "Clarksdale" type found at other sites thought to have been visited by De Soto, have been found in the Carden Bottoms locality near Dardanelle, and a sixteenth century site recently excavated near Little Rock was tentatively identified by archeologists as Tunican. Finally, a map drawn in 1673 by the French explorer Father Jacques Marquette indicates Tunicans were still living along the Arkansas River at that date.

The southeastern Arkansas province of Guachoya has also been considered Tunican. A number of archeological sites in that region have produced early sixteenth century ceramics that closely resemble slightly later ceramics from sites in western Mississippi definitely linked with Tunica Indians. Late seventeenth century French accounts also mention Tunican groups along the lower Ouachita River in Arkansas as well as near Bayou Bartholomew in extreme southeast Arkansas near the Louisiana state line.

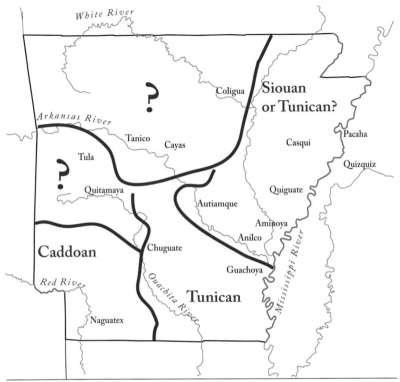

Sixteenth century culture areas in Arkansas

Most debate concerns the cultural identity of sixteenth century groups inhabiting the lower Arkansas River Valley and adjacent portions of northeastern Arkansas. One hypothesis suggests that the sixteenth century provinces of Casqui and Pacaha were ancestral to later Quapaw Indians. The Quapaws are Siouan speakers who were living in four villages around the confluence of the Arkansas and Mississippi when French explorers began to descend the Mississippi River in the late seventeenth century. There are similarities in ceramics found on late prehistoric sites in northeast Arkansas and sixteenth century sites along the lower Arkansas River. On the basis of this evidence, some archeologists suggest that the four Quapaw villages visited by late seventeenth century Frenchmen represent the remnants of more populous ancestral societies that were shattered as a consequence of De Soto's invasion.

Other archeologists, however, point out that the style and construction of late prehistoric and sixteenth century houses found on sites in northeastern Arkansas and along the lower Arkansas River, which were square with mud-plastered or mat-covered walls, differ significantly from those built by seventeenth century Quapaws, which were very long (to shelter several families) and had bark covered walls. These archeologists question the Quapaw cultural affiliation attributed to late prehistoric and sixteenth century sites in eastern Arkansas. They suggest that the Quapaws were immigrants who came into the lower Arkansas River Valley area after the departure of the Spaniards in 1543.

This alternative hypothesis is based on a Quapaw migration tradition related in 1820 to George Izard by Paheka, the grandfather of Heckaton, who was principal chief of the Quapaws at the time. This tradition tells of the Quapaws coming into Arkansas from homelands in the lower Ohio River Valley. Reaching the St. Francis River, they drove away Indians called the "Tonnikas," and after reaching the Arkansas River they drove away "Intouka" Indians, whom the whites of the period called Illinois. Support for this hypothesis comes from study of the Quapaw language, which linguists regard as a "pure" dialect—that is, having no borrowed words or structures that might be expected in the language of a group coalesced from the remnants of earlier populations. Furthermore, the Indian words and names recorded in the De Soto accounts when the Spaniards were in northeast Arkansas are most likely Tunican, not Siouan (although it cannot be determined if these terms were used by the Indians then living in northeastern Arkansas, or if they were used by some of De Soto's native guides who crossed the Mississippi River with him).

If the Quapaws were immigrants who arrived in the region only after the departure of De Soto, then who were the Indians the Spaniards encountered in northeastern Arkansas? The Tunican words recorded in the De Soto accounts for northeastern Arkansas lead some to suggest that these Indians too were Tunican. But, if northeastern Arkansas is added to the more widely accepted six-teenth century Tunican domains of western Mississippi and central and southeastern Arkansas, a very large region is created within which considerable variation in ceramics styles—archeologists' favorite cultural marker—is found. Furthermore, bioarcheological studies of human skeletal remains from a few sixteenth century sites show that these central Arkansas River Valley populations were genetically different from late prehistoric populations in northeastern Arkansas as well as from Caddoan populations in southwestern Arkansas.

Clearly, there is a need for much more archeological and bio-archeological research in Arkansas before all questions concerning sixteenth century cultural identities can be answered.

Consequences of First Contacts

The activities of early Spanish explorers had tragic conse-quences for native peoples of southeastern North America. The effects of battles with the Spaniards and of enslavement took a toll upon native populations. The introduction of Old World diseases against which the Indians had no immunity—smallpox, tuberculosis, plague, typhus, influenza, yellow fever, measles, and possibly malaria and mumps—resulted in many additional deaths. When French explorers visited Arkansas at the end of the seventeenth century, the populous, well-organized towns the Spaniards had visited in the northeastern part of the state were gone.

These effects of contact with Europeans were compounded by environmental changes. Recent tree ring studies provide evidence of severe droughts that began to affect eastern Arkansas at the time of De Soto's invasion and intensified for several decades thereafter. The combination of population reduction and other cultural and environmental stresses upon sixteenth century societies must have resulted in a tremendous loss of many important elements of culture. Disproportionate numbers of deaths among elderly people who were responsible for passing on important cultural traditions, and among the young who would carry on these traditions, dealt fatal blows both to the heritage of the past and the hope for the future among many native groups.

These consequences of contact with Europeans were not felt uniformly throughout the Southeast, nor even throughout Arkansas. Old World diseases like smallpox and tuberculosis would have had the most devastating effects upon large, concentrated populations such as those living in the central Mississippi Valley. In the Caddo area, where populations were more dispersed, Old World diseases would have had much less impact. Bioarcheological studies indicate that this indeed was the case. In all areas where Europeans had either direct or indirect contacts with indigenous populations, the world of the Indians was changed dramatically and forever.

3

TRADITIONS:
Seventeenth and Eighteenth
Century Lifeways

Several Indian groups lived in what is now Arkansas during the seventeenth and eighteenth centuries. Quapaws occupied lands around the confluence of the Mississippi and Arkansas rivers, Caddo villages were distributed throughout the Red and Ouachita river drainages, and Tunicas and Koroas inhabited the Mississippi Valley region of central and southeastern Arkansas. Osage Indians, whose main villages were along tributaries of the Missouri River, controlled a vast territory that included much of northern Arkansas. By the eighteenth century, the Tunicas and Koroas had vacated their Arkansas homeland and relocated in what is now the state of Louisiana.

The remaining groups were removed from their homelands during the nineteenth century to reservations in Indian Territory (now Oklahoma and Kansas) and were largely ignored by nineteenth and early twentieth century anthropologists. In order to produce sketches of the traditional lifeways of these Indians, it is necessary to rely upon observations recorded by colonial era explorers and settlers. In contrast to the chroniclers of the De Soto expedition, who frequently identified Southeastern Indians by names that did not survive into later centuries, writers of the seventeenth and eighteenth centuries more often identified Indian tribes by names that are still used by their descendants today.

During the 130-year interval separating the 1543 departure of De Soto expedition survivors and the 1673 arrival of Marquette and Jolliet, tremendous changes occurred both in native population distributions and in native lifeways. Since we know very little about what transpired during this undocumented interval, this period is often referred to as the "protohistoric dark ages." As mentioned in the preceding section, the combined effects of disease, warfare, enslavement, and drought, all of which accompanied contacts with Europeans in the sixteenth century, make it very difficult for modern scholars to establish connections between the groups identified by De Soto and groups that were present in the Southeast in later times. Indeed, many groups encountered by De Soto probably did not survive the protohistoric dark ages. The reconstructions of Indian cultures provided in this chapter, based on seventeenth and eighteenth century accounts, should probably not be extended backward to represent the cultural characteristics of sixteenth century tribes.

The Quapaws

The Quapaws, or O-gah-pah, belong to the Dhegiha subdivision of the Siouan language family and are closely related to the Osage, Omaha, Kansa, and Ponca tribes, all of whom speak similar dialects. In 1673 Marquette and Jolliet traveled down the Mississippi River and visited a Quapaw village located on the west bank of the Mississippi a few miles above its confluence with the Arkansas River. In 1682 René-Robert Cavelier, Sieur de La Salle, visited the same village and three others: one located on the east side of the Mississippi, one near the confluence, and one several miles up the Arkansas. Beginning with these early contacts, the Quapaws became allies of the French, the Spanish, and later the Americans. During the nineteenth century the Quapaws were forced to give up their Arkansas homelands. They were removed first to the Red River Valley and later to Indian Territory. They persisted in spite

Marquette and Joliet at Chicago August 1673.

Sketch by Charles Peck of Chicago, published by Rufus Blanchard, Chicago (courtesy of the State Historical Society of Wisconsin, WHi[x3]10791)

of these difficulties and today proudly celebrate their distinctive cultural heritage.

When first encountered by the French, the Quapaws recognized the existence of a powerful force called Wakondah that permeated the world and held everything in balance. According to their belief, Wakondah was created when primordial male and female life forces were joined. This event occurred in the very distant past, before people emerged from the womb of the earth to live upon its surface. The Quapaws recognized the existence of other forces, including the sun, the moon, and thunder. Plants and animals also possessed spiritual qualities, and certain animals served as guardian spirits whose wisdom and power could aid individuals who adopted them.

Ceremonies were held at various times of the year to observe events important in the life of Quapaw communities. Examples include a planting ceremony held in the spring, and a Green Corn (or Busk) ceremony held in the summer to give thanks for the crops that were soon to be harvested. Offerings of gifts and prayers to various deities and to the sacred forces of nature were part of these ceremonies, along with feasting, dancing, contests, and other acts of public celebration.

Shamans (religious practitioners who possessed special abilities to send their souls into the spirit realm) were responsible for curing people of illnesses, and several curing societies existed, each with a different animal guardian spirit. Curing society members selected promising initiates who underwent a long apprenticeship before they were formally inducted. Specialists who maintained the tribe's oral history and extensive genealogical information also performed rituals associated with the passage of individuals through crucial life stages. The most important of these were children's naming ceremonies, marriage celebrations, and funeral rites. These ceremonies ensured that significant events in people's lives were properly endowed with the power of Wakondah.

Sometimes rituals were performed to serve other needs that arose within the community. For example, the men of each village would gather in the spring and sit in a circle. Fatherless children could choose an adoptive father from among them. This individual would then assume responsiblity for their care.

Quapaw society was organized in terms of statuses derived from ancestry and relationships based on marriage. Every member of Quapaw society belonged to a descent group traced through his or her father's line. The kin terms used by the Quapaws reinforced the importance of these groups. For example, uncles and cousins on the father's side were distinguished by terms that differed from those used to designate uncles and cousins on the mother's side. In modern American society, "uncle" and "cousin" are designated by terms that do not distinguish the mother's or father's side. Identification with a particular generation or even a particular family was less important among the Quapaws than membership in a descent group.

Descent groups were organized into 21 named clans. Following the rule of patrilineal descent (that is, tracing ancestry through the father's line), each person belonged to his or her father's clan. Each clan adopted a guardian spirit—usually an animal or some

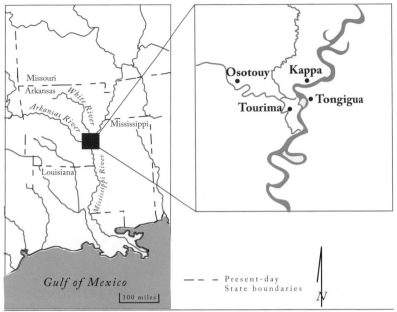

locations of the Quapaw Indians in the late seventeenth century

element of nature, such as lightning—and these guardian spirits conferred on each clan the right to perform specific rituals. Although the names of only a few Quapaw clans have been preserved, we know that the 21 clans were divided into two groups called Sky People and Earth People. Clans representing the Earth People performed rituals that helped sustain the physical and material well-being of the community. Clans representing the Sky People performed rituals that concerned spiritual affairs, especially relations with important spirit beings.

The Sky People and Earth People division also regulated marriage. A person could not marry someone who belonged to the same division. Consequently, everyone's inlaws came from the opposite division as their patrilinial, or clan, relatives. The relationship between the two intermarrying divisions symbolized the productive power of male and female life forces and the continuity of the tribe through successive generations.

Each Quapaw village had a leader whose office was inherited through the male line. Although leaders were held in esteem, they did not rule in an autocratic manner. Each village leader was assisted by a council of male elders. Leaders usually presided at village councils, at war councils, and at various other ceremonies. Village councils were held in large council houses called longhouses (even today), where the participants were seated according to rank. The leader and elders occupied positions of highest honor, followed by warriors and then everyone else. Each village made decisions concerning only its own affairs, except in cases where larger matters that concerned the entire tribe were under consideration. In such cases, a tribal or intervillage consensus was sought.

Quapaw villages contained several longhouses, each occupied by several families, arranged around an open central plaza. The council house stood near the plaza, where there was also a partially enclosed, elevated platform on which the leader and other important people sat during public ceremonies. Longhouses were constructed by driving parallel rows of long poles into the ground. The tops of the poles were pulled toward the center, forming an arch and tied together in pairs. This framework was strengthened by horizonal withes and covered with sheets of bark. Platforms for sitting and sleeping were constructed along the inner walls and at the ends of the structures. Hearths placed along the midline of the interior were used by the individual families. Quapaw villages had a sacred temple in which priests performed ceremonies. Seventeenth century French accounts indicate that these temples stood on man-made, flat-topped mounds.

The Quapaws were sedentary farmers who raised corn, beans, squash, gourds, melons, and tobacco in fields—some quite large—scattered among the villages. The Quapaws also cultivated peach trees, which were introduced in Florida by sixteenth century Spanish settlers and then spread to other regions.

Agricultural products were supplemented by wild plant foods including fruits, nuts, seeds, and roots. Hunting and fishing were also important. Deer, bear, and buffalo were sought for meat, hides, and other products. Small mammals, turkeys, and waterfowl were also

A Quapaw village scene by Kugee Supernaw, a Quapaw artist (courtesy of the artist)

taken. Dogs and European-introduced chickens and horses were kept as domestic animals. Dogs were killed and eaten on certain ritual occasions.

Quapaw women were in charge of gardening. Women also butchered animals captured in the chase and prepared the hides, gathered wood and wild foods, cooked food, cared for the children, and performed household chores. The agricultural cycle was marked by a series of important rituals, some of which served to honor and sanctify the activities performed by women.

Men hunted, fished, waged war, and managed community and political affairs. Positions of political and religious leadership were held exclusively by men. Various rituals, often quite elaborate, were performed in preparation for warfare and hunting. Important religious ceremonies, such as the Green Corn ceremony, required extensive preparations including rites to purify the participants. The deliberations of village councils were also preceded by acts of ritual purification (which often included taking sweatbaths or "washing" the body with smoke from a special fire), since these too were regarded as sacred affairs.

Quapaw women wore deerskin skirts that reached from the waist to the knees. Married women wore their hair loose, while unmarried women wore their hair in two braids that were rolled into coils secured behind each ear and decorated with ornaments. Men wore buckskin loincloths, leggings, moccasins, and shirts. They also decorated themselves with tattoos and with strings of beads in their ears and noses. Buffalo robes were worn during the winter. For ceremonies, Quapaws painted their bodies red and black and wore headdresses decorated with feathers, buffalo horns, or animal furs. Decorated wooden masks were used for some ceremonies.

The material culture of the Quapaws was undoubtedly quite elaborate but unfortunately we know very little about it. In addition to the clothing items already mentioned, early historic accounts furnish information on a few other objects. Mats woven of cane were used to cover sitting and sleeping platforms in houses. On some occasions chiefs and other important individuals sat on mountain lion skins. Quapaw women wove baskets and were excellent potters. Most baskets and pottery vessels were used for storage or food preparation and consumption, although some were undoubtedly used in ritual contexts as well. Wooden platters were also made, some of which were traded to other tribes. Dugout canoes were a means of transportation. The bow and arrow was used for hunting, and spears were used for fishing from the dugouts. Music for ceremonies was provided by gourd rattles and drums made of pots over which deer skins were stretched.

Relations with other tribes consisted either of warfare with enemies, or alliances created for the purposes of friendship, trade, or to wage war against a common enemy.

Preparations for war involved elaborate rituals to ensure that the powers of Wakondah would accompany the warriors into battle. When a village chief and his council of advisors decided to send out a war party, a public announcement was made. Warriors who wished to participate took a stick from the chief, which served to seal the commitment of the warrior and to guarantee his subsequent reward (returning warriors gained honor from their exploits and usually received a share of any booty that was taken). Next, a war club was

Quapaw warriors marching to attack an enemy village. A. Antoine de Saint-Gervais, *Nouvel album de peoples on collection de tableaux* (Paris, 1835), p. 100.

painted red, the color symbolizing war and bloodshed (and also the color associated with poisonous insects and reptiles), and placed at the edge of the enemy's territory. Meanwhile, village leaders enlisted allies from other tribes and preparations were made for a feast and a dance in which the painted warriors acted out the anticipated battle. The war leader, who meanwhile was fasting and undergoing purification rites, made a final speech to inspire his followers before their departure. During the early historic period, the Quapaws took scalps or prisoners from the settlements they raided. The women of each village determined the fate of captives brought back by the warriors. Some captives might be selected to take the place of deceased relatives, some might become slaves, and some might be put to death. The Quapaws also sold captured enemies into the European slave trade.

Alliances with other groups, Indian or European, were made by means of the calumet ceremony. The calumet, or "peace pipe," was a two-piece object consisting of a decorated wooden stick, about two feet long, attached to a pipebowl carved of red pipestone, or catlinite. The calumet ceremony was a very elaborate affair, involving feasting, dancing, gift exchanges, and, of course, passing the calumet for all of the participants to smoke. This ceremony served to create kinshiplike relations between the participants, so that allies would be bound by sacred obligations toward one another. The creation of these alliances was consistent with Quapaw belief that the powers of Wakondah infused all significant events and relationships in life. Those who shared the calumet sent aloft, with the smoke, their wish to be joined as if they were kin. By creating such relationships, the Quapaws "adopted" their allies into positions vacated by important or well-remembered people who were deceased. Thus both the kinship relation and the tribe as a whole were renewed.

It is important to recognize that the calumet ceremony served as the primary means by which Quapaws interacted with Europeans and Americans during much of the historic era. As a consequence, their relations with European and American allies were strongly influenced by the obligations and expectations this sacred ceremony conferred on its participants.

The Osages

The Osage or Wa-sha-she Indians also belong to the Dhegiha subdivision of the Siouan language family, and are closely related to the Quapaw, Omaha, Kansa, and Ponca tribes. French explorers in the early eighteenth century visited the Osages on the Missouri and Osage rivers in southwestern Missouri. Their seasonal hunting and trading forays brought them annually into northern Arkansas. The following ethnographic sketch is drawn primarily from early nineteenth century sources, since earlier French and Spanish accounts provide only scanty information on Osage culture.

The Osage Indians called themselves "Children of the Middle Waters." Wakondah, the creative force of their universe, separated

"Calumet," from the journal of Minet (courtesy of the National Archives of Canada, C-11012) air, earth, and water from the original middle waters and created things on the earth. The major components of the universe were sky and earth, and night and day. Living beings were put on the earth's surface, which separated the sky above from the womb of the earth below. Night and day represented everlasting cycles through which all living things passed. Osages trace their origin to a time long ago when two groups of people, called the Sky People and the Earth People, came together. The Sky People descended into the world newly conceived by Wakondah and there met the Earth People, whom they joined to create the Osage tribe.

Like the Quapaws, the Osages traced their ancestry through the father's line and organized their communities by clans making up the Sky People and Earth People divisions. Each clan appointed representatives to participate in village and tribal councils, which performed the main tasks of government and also advised the two tribal chiefs—one representing each division. The chief of the Sky People was responsible for all matters related to peace, while the chief of the Earth People was responsible for all matters concerning war.

Osage villages were organized with reference to the major dimensions of the universe. Houses were arranged on either side of a main road running east to west, which symbolized the earth's surface between the sky above and the earth below. Two village chiefs, each representing one of the main tribal divisions, lived in the center of the village on opposite sides of the main road. The clans of the Sky People lived on the same side of the road as their chief, and the clans of the Earth People were arranged on the opposite side, with their chief.

Most houses were rectangular and were constructed in the same manner as Quapaw houses. The completed house frames were covered with buffalo hides, sheets of bark, or woven mats. They had smoke holes in the roofs and doors opening to the east (the chief's house had two doors, one at either end). Some were quite large (as much as 100 feet long), accommodating several closely related families. Sometimes smaller circular-shaped buildings were constructed either for use as dwellings or as sweat lodges (places where fires could

Locations of the Osage Indians in the late seventeenth century

be stoked for sweat baths, a common method of ritual purification). In permanent villages, special lodges were constructed for village council meetings and rituals.

In the early nineteenth century the Osage people were divided into five major groups, called bands, each of which had its own village. The pattern of village life was ordered in large part by customs that were maintained by a group of male elders known as the Little Old Men. These elders were responsible for establishing standards of appropriate conduct, advising the village leaders, making important decisions affecting tribal affairs in times of peace and war, and maintaining sacred knowledge and traditions. To attain the ranks of the Little Old Men, serious-minded individuals underwent lengthy instruction, which began during childhood. Individuals could pass through as many as seven degrees of learning, at each degree acquiring familiarity with a particular body of sacred knowledge.

Marriages were arranged by families. The parents of a young man typically selected his wife. Husbands and wives belonged to opposite tribal divisions and usually came from different villages. Gifts were brought to the young woman's family by the young man's family. These gifts were kept if the marriage proposal was acceptable and returned if not. Sometimes an Osage man would take his first wife's sisters as additional wives. Since inheritance passed through the male line, a man would often marry his deceased brother's widow so that he could provide for his brother's children.

The Osages hunted, gathered, and gardened to provide themselves with food and raw materials. Men were responsible for hunting, while women had primary responsibility for gardening and gathering. Corn, beans, squashes, and pumpkins were grown in gardens surrounding the villages. Various wild plant foods, including fruits, berries, nuts, and edible roots, were gathered. Plant foods—domestic and wild—were usually dried and stored for later use.

Hunting was much more important than gardening in the Osage economy and annual cycle. Bison, deer, and elk were the animals most often hunted, although bear and smaller animals were also taken. Hides and other items acquired in the hunt were sometimes used as trade goods.

In springtime, fields were cleared along river bottoms adjacent to the village. Women from each family tended their own plots until the plants were sufficiently established to thrive on their own. During summer, residents of several villages gathered together in large camps and traveled west to Kansas and Nebraska to hunt buffalo. The bow and arrow was the primary hunting weapon. When horses became available in the eighteenth century, a shift to mounted hunting took place. In autumn, people returned to their villages to harvest the ripened crops. People from several villages gathered again in the fall to hunt buffalo and deer in favorite areas. Northern Arkansas was one area often used by the Osage during early historic times. Winters were spent in the villages, the people living on stored garden produce and animals taken locally. A late winter or early spring

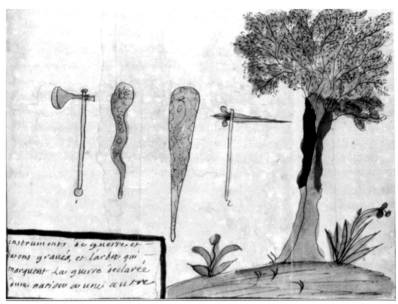

"Instruments of War," by François Dumont de Montigny, ca. 1747, Ayer Collection Ms. 257 (courtesy of the Newberry Library, Chicago)

hunt for beaver and bear took families away from their villages once again, until it was time to return for spring planting.

Osage men were responsible not only for hunting, but also for waging war and for defending villages against enemies. They also managed the political affairs of the tribe. Men shaved their heads, leaving only a scalplock, or roach extending from the forehead to the back of the neck. Different scalplock designs were worn to identify clan membership. Deerskin loincloths, leggings, and moccasins were worn, and bearskin or buffalo robes were added in cold weather. Ornaments were worn in the ears and on the arms, and warriors tattooed their chests and arms. Designs were painted on the body for ceremonial occasions.

Women were responsible for a wide variety of activities in addition to planting and tending gardens and preparing meals. Houses were constructed by women, as were most of the interior furnishings and utensils. Hideworking and manufacture of skin clothing were important activities. Women also wove sashes, belts, neckbands, and cords from buffalo hair or nettle weed fiber. Some of these were decorated for use in important religious and social ceremonies.

Women wore their hair long and loose. They wore deerskin dresses cinched at the waist with woven belts, leggings, and moccasins. Jewelry consisted of earrings, pendants, and bracelets, and many women decorated their bodies with elaborate tattoos. Ceremonial garments were decorated with bits of ermine and puma fur. Clothing was often perfumed with chewed columbine seed. Osage women wore scented powder and perfume made from certain flowers, and enhanced their complexions by rubbing the dried pulp of pumpkins into their skin.

Child rearing was the responsibility of the family, clan, and village. Fathers instructed their sons in the skills of hunting and warfare, while mothers taught their daughters how to tend crops and manage domestic affairs. Values and important social and religious beliefs were learned from elders. Each child was carefully nurtured so the Osage way of life would persist through succeeding generations.

The Caddos

The Caddo Indians were another major group inhabiting Arkansas during the early historic period. Several communities around the great bend of the Red River in southwest Arkansas and eastern Texas comprised the Kadohadacho alliance. To the south, in present-day Louisiana, were the villages of the Natchitoches alliance and farther to the west along the upper Angelina and Neches rivers in east Texas were the villages of the Hasinai alliance. The Cahinnio Indians, who were allies of the Kadohadacho in the seventeenth century, occupied the Ouachita River drainage in western Arkansas.

The Kadohadacho, Natchitoches, and Hasinai alliances consisted of autonomous local communities connected through diplomatic ties. These groups, plus the Cahinnio, represent the southern core of Caddo-speaking peoples. They spoke similar dialects and

"Tattooed Wichita Woman," by Hal Story (courtesy of the Texas Memorial Museum)

were distantly related to Plains Caddo linguistic groups including the Wichitas, Pawnees, Arikaras, and Kitsais. Occupying the area between the northern borderlands of New Spain and the Mississippi Valley, the southern Caddos played a pivotal role during the colonial era in the contests for empire between France and Spain. The westward spread of American settlement eventually encroached upon their domain, and in the nineteenth century most Caddos were forced to relocate on reservations in Indian Territory.

Several creation stories tell how the Caddo world came into existence. The Kadohadachos traced their origins to a cave in a hill named Chakanina (or "place of crying"), out of which came an old man from the underworld bringing fire, a pipe, and a drum. The old man's wife accompanied him, bringing corn and pumpkin seeds.

Others followed, both people and animals, but before they could all make their escape Wolf closed the cave's entrance, trapping forever those who remained below. The people on the surface wept bitterly for those left behind.

Another story, recorded by a Spanish priest who worked among the Hasinais in eastern Texas, relates the origin of the Supreme Being, Ayo-Caddi-Aymay, or "Captain of the Sky." In this story a pregnant woman was killed by a serpent monster with horns reaching up to the sky. The woman's sister escaped the monster and later brought her mother to the scene of the murder. The women found a drop of the pregnant sister's blood in an acorn shell, which they took back to their house. During the night the blood turned into a tiny boy, about the size of a finger, and the next night the boy grew into a full-sized young man. The grandmother made him a bow and arrows. When he learned of his mother's fate, the young man avenged her death by killing the monster with an arrow. With his grandmother and aunt he ascended to the sky to become Ayo-Caddi-Aymay.

Ayo-Caddi-Aymay was considered the most powerful spirit being, with authority over lesser spirit beings and forces that also affected the daily lives of the Caddos. A series of rituals were performed to maintain favorable relations between the Caddos and the spirit world. These rituals served to organize the annual cycle. The most important events were related to agriculture. In spring there was a forecasting ceremony, in which priests contacted the spirit beings to obtain information about the coming year. A planting ceremony honored the women as they began their work in the fields—activities that were considered sacred among the Caddos. A first fruits ceremony was performed later in the summer as the crops began to ripen. A harvest ceremony in the fall was the largest celebration of the year, in which thanks were given for the years' crops and other rites were performed to reinforce the solidarity of the local group. Other important activities that occurred during the year, including housebuilding, warfare, trade, and births, marriages, and deaths, were similarly celebrated with appropriate rituals.

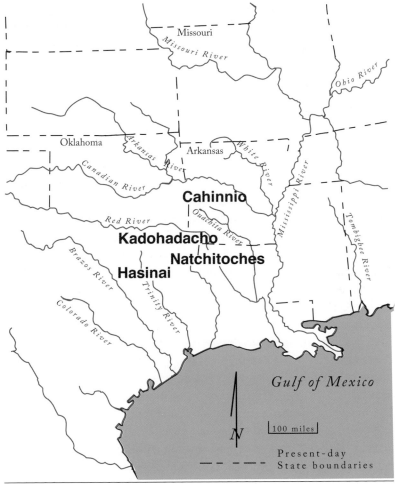

Locations of the Caddo in the seventeenth century

Caddo social organization is imperfectly understood but some information can be gleaned from early European accounts. Each household consisted of several families related through the female line. Individuals also belonged to clans and usually married someone who belonged to a different clan. Some clans were ranked according to the relative strength of the animal after which they were named (e.g., Bison, Bear, Panther, Wolf, and Beaver). Children belonged to their mother's clan unless the father belonged to a "stronger" clan than the mother, in which case the man's sons became members of his clan.

Political organization was based on a hierarchy of offices. Among the Hasinais, and perhaps for other groups as well, leadership at the community level was vested in the office of the caddi, who held authority in numerous civic and religious affairs. Upon the death of this leader, the office would pass to the eldest son or closest male heir. Other officials known as conchas, chayas, and tanmas assisted the caddi in community matters such as house construction and preparation of fields. Shamans and a class of medicine men known as connas performed a variety of rituals including blessing food and treating illnesses. Other high-ranking individuals formed a council of advisors that assisted the caddi. At the level of the alliance, a head priest known as the xinesi possessed the utmost authority in both civil and religious affairs. The xinesi was held in very high esteem, and community members provided for his material needs.

Early European visitors described Caddo settlements as "cantons." Each consisted of several family farmsteads dispersed at intervals along a river or stream. Some of these communities stretched for miles. Each family chose a site of sufficient size to build houses and plant crops. A typical farmstead consisted of one or two thatched, beehive-shaped houses along with an elevated corn crib, an outdoor work platform, and log mortars for pounding corn into meal. Fields and woodlots surrounded the farmsteads.

House construction and the clearing and planting of fields were communal activities. When a new house was needed, the caddi set a date for the event. He dispatched his tanmas to notify members of the local community and to assign to each person certain responsibilities. If an individual received a token stick, for example, then he was responsible for cutting and trimming a pole that would serve as a wall post. Others gathered saplings to be laced crosswise into the framework or made thongs to secure the laths. Women gathered bundles of long grass to thatch the walls and roof. On the morning of the appointed day the caddi took his seat in a place of honor, from which he directed the work. Men who had cut wall posts set them into holes they had previously dug, forming a circle of uprights. A center post with a forked upper end was set in the middle of the circle, and two short pieces of wood were fastened at the top to form a crosspiece. Two men using rope nooses drew the tops of the wall posts together and tied them to the crosspiece. Next, the horizontal laths were woven through the wall posts and secured to the frame with bark thongs. Grass thatch was added to cover the structure from bottom to top, with a grass figure crowning the completed dome. The final construction step was the removal of the center post. Since several families might occupy a single house, these structures were often quite large, measuring as much as 60 feet in diameter.

The entire process was usually finished in a single day. Upon completion, a shaman recited a blessing and a feast of venison and corn gruel was shared by all the participants.

The central interior feature of the Caddo house was a hearth fed by four large logs oriented to the cardinal directions and lit from an ember brought from the fire in the village's sacred temple. The sense of community that nearby families shared derived in part from this common use of the sacred fire to light family hearths. At the rear and along either side of the interior were the family quarters. There were apparently no partitions separating them, but each contained sleeping platforms made of woven cane mats supported by a pole framework and elevated 3 or 4 feet above the floor. Buffalo robes covered the mats. Additional mats—some decorated with brightly colored designs—were arched over the platforms to create alcoves. Storage platforms or lofts, where food supplies and utensils were kept, were built along the walls opposite or adjacent to the sleeping quarters. Although each family maintained its own supplies, the central fire was shared and common meals were prepared with contributions made by each family. A head woman of the household supervised most domestic activities.

Most Caddos were sedentary farmers who planted fields of corn, beans, pumpkins, squashes, watermelons, sunflowers, and tobacco. Family fields were cleared adjacent to the scattered houses, although, as with housebuilding, the spring preparation of fields was a community undertaking. When the time came for the crops to be planted, the residents of a community, including the caddi (who again served as the overseer of the work detail), gathered at one family's farmstead to clear the ground and prepare the soil. A pick made by tying a pointed bone or sharp, fire-hardened piece of wood to a wooden handle was used for this activity. Ground breaking at a farmstead was generally finished by late morning. As this work was going on, the family whose fields were being cleared would prepare a feast to be shared later that day. The rest of the day was devoted to games and socializing. Each farmstead's fields were worked in turn until all of the planting was done.

Hunting for buffalo, bear, deer, and smaller mammals and birds was important, as were fishing and gathering shellfish, nuts, berries, seeds, and edible roots. The bow, typically made of the strong and resilient wood of the Osage orange or bois d'arc tree, was the main hunting weapon. Arrows were made of cane with a sharpened fire-hardened tip or a stone point at the end. Hunters sometimes disguised themselves to resemble the animals they were hunting and decoys were sometimes used.

Most food was cooked. Green corn ears were roasted; otherwise corn as well as seeds, nuts, and some roots were parched on hot coals and ground into flour. The flour could then be mixed with water or bear oil and eaten cold or boiled to make gruel. Other foodstuffs, including squash, beans, and pieces of meat, could be added to the gruel to make a heartier stew. Flour could also be mixed with water and formed into loaves which were baked on hot stone slabs. Meat was usually boiled in a broth.

Caddos living near salt marshes, or salines, made salt by boiling the briny water in large, shallow clay pans. The salt remaining in the pans after the water evaporated was stored for later use or for trade. In addition to salt, the Caddos traded other materials, including bear oil or grease and the wood of the Osage orange tree, prized for the manufacture of bows.

"Saltmaking," watercolor by Dan Kerlin (courtesy of the University of Arkansas Museum)

Caddos were well known for their pottery, baskets, woven mats, and dressed skins. Pottery was often decorated with intricate designs. Vessels were created in many shapes, including platters, bowls, jars, and bottles, to serve various storage, food preparation, and eating needs. Commodities for trade, such as salt and bear oil, were transported in pottery vessels. Some vessels were used for rituals.

Women made highly decorated baskets and mats woven from cane splints. Baskets served domestic as well as ritual needs. Sacred objects stored in temples were kept in specially made, lidded baskets. Woven mats were used as floor and bench coverings in houses and in temples. Mats specially woven by women working under the supervision of an elderly matron were offered in the sacred fire temple to Ayo-Caddi-Aymay in preparation for the annual planting ceremony.

Clothing worn during the early historic period by Caddo men included breechcloths and moccasins, to which wraps made of deer

"A Caddo Village Scene," by Hal Story (courtesy of the Texas Memorial Museum)

skins or buffalo hides were added during cold weather. Women wore skirts made of deerskins or woven matting. In warm weather they went topless, but when it was cold a heavier skin wrap was worn. Deerskin shirts, exquisitely decorated with fringes and colored and beaded designs, were sometimes worn by women and men. For religious ceremonies, special deerskin garments bearing brightly colored decorations were worn.

Caddo men kept their hair trimmed short, except for a long lock which sometimes was braided or decorated with feathers or shell ornaments. Caddo women wore their long hair braided and tied close to the head. Both men and women had tattoos, although women evidently were more enthusiastic about this than the men, frequently decorating their faces, arms, and torsos with elaborate designs. Men and women painted designs on their faces and bodies for religious ceremonies.

Warfare was an important means by which southern Caddos maintained the integrity of their territory against pressures from the Apaches to the west and the Osages and various Plains tribes to the north. War expeditions were undertaken to seek revenge for deaths or other insults committed by neighboring tribes. When the leaders of a Caddo community wished to organize a war party, ambassadors bearing requests for support or assistance were sent to allied communities. Once a war party was organized, an elaborate series of rituals was performed. Offerings were made to supernatural beings to gain their sanction and enlist their support. Other ceremonies and various contests served to sharpen the physical capabilities of the warriors and whip up their fervor. Throughout these proceedings the warriors were segregated from the rest of the community. Often a funeral ceremony was performed prior to the departure of the warriors so their souls would travel unimpeded to the afterworld, should they be killed in battle.

Funeral ceremonies consisted of a series of rituals intended to facilitate the travel of a dead person's soul to the afterworld. First, the body was washed and dressed in fine clothes. Three priests presided over the funeral. Two of them chanted and placed offerings of tobacco and bows and arrows upon an empty wooden coffin. While the grave was being dug, the body was placed in the coffin along with articles required in the afterlife. Then an elder priest gave the eulogy. As the coffin was carried to the grave, arrows were shot into the air to warn the keeper of the House of Death that the dead person's soul soon would arrive. Offerings of food were placed on the grave after burial and were replenished over the next several days until the family was certain the soul had begun its journey. According to Caddo belief, the soul traveled first west and then south through the heavens, finally arriving at the House of Death, where it would reside for eternity. Existence in the House of Death was considered pleasant, free from the difficulties people often experienced during life in this world.

The organization of Caddo communities into hierarchically ranked classes of people—commoners, lower-level civil officers, and high ranking civil/religious leaders—provided a framework for interaction with Europeans during much of the historic period. When European travelers approached Caddo villages, they were usually met by a contingent sent out to greet them along the path. The leaders of the Europeans would be escorted to the dwelling of the caddi, or to a specially erected ceremonial structure, and seated in a place of honor. Sharing the calumet served to create a bond of friendship between the two sets of leaders that extended to other members of their groups. In this way, Caddos attempted to incorporate Europeans within their own social system.

Tunicas and Koroas

When Hernando de Soto and his army reached the Mississippi River in the spring of 1541, the Indians they encountered in the province of Quizquiz, in present-day northwest Mississippi and southwest Tennessee, were probably Tunica speakers. The Tunica language is distinctive among Southeastern Indian languages but seems most closely related to the Muskogean family. In the sixteenth century, Tunica Indians occupied a large region extending along both sides of the Mississippi River in northwest Mississippi and eastern Arkansas. In the late seventeenth century, French explorers and missionaries reported Tunica Indians and the closely related Koroa Indians (who probably spoke a Tunica dialect) living along the Arkansas and Ouachita rivers and along the Mississippi River south of the Arkansas. By 1699 most Tunicas had relocated their villages along the lower stretch of the Yazoo River in present-day Mississippi. Within a few more years the Koroas had been severely reduced and remnants of that tribe had also moved to the lower Yazoo region. In the aftermath of the Natchez Rebellion of 1729, the few remaining Koroas dispersed among the Chickasaws and the Natchez. Meanwhile, the Tunicas relocated several more times, ending up, at the turn of the nineteenth century, with Biloxi Indians near Marksville, Louisiana, where they remain today.

Historic accounts of Tunica and Koroa Indians are sparse and fragmentary, but we can identify characteristics that are both similar to and different from other Southeastern tribes.

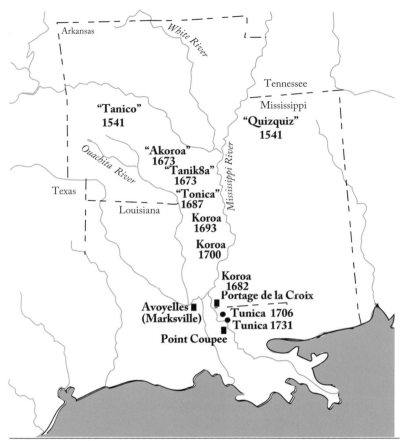

Locations of the Tunicas from the sixteenth to eighteenth centuries (terms in quotations reflect original spellings on maps; the 8 in Tanik8a is a vowel symbol used in Spanish manuscripts)

Like all Southeastern Indians, the Tunicas recognized spiritual qualities in many aspects of nature. Prominent were the sun, thunder and fire, heaven and earth, and the sacred directions (east, north, south, and west). The Tunicas, however, attributed a female identity to the sun—considered male by many other groups. They also recognized fire as a deity in its own right, not merely the earthly symbol of the sun's power, as many other Southeastern Indians believed. Each village contained a sacred fire temple in which religious specialists performed their rituals. One Frenchman saw small statues of a woman and a frog in one temple. The woman may have symbolized the sun or upper world, while the frog probably symbolized the underworld, as it generally did among Southeastern Indians.

We know very little about the social life of the Tunicas. Leaders apparently inherited their offices. In the eighteenth century separate leaders were responsible for civil affairs and warfare. This may have been the case during earlier times as well, although no specific mention of it is found in earlier European accounts. Warriors achieved distinction for exploits in battle, which entitled them to wear elaborate tattoos. Some men had several wives, a practice that was not uncommon among Southeastern tribes. Upon death, people were buried with items required in the afterworld. One French visitor wrote that games, dances, and feasts were often held in the open plazas of Koroa villages.

Houses were circular, built of upright posts interwoven with cane laths. Walls were plastered with clay, and the dome-shaped roofs were covered with grass thatch. Small doorways provided the only source of natural light and the only exit for the smoke of small fires lit inside to provide light and warmth. A member of La Salle's 1682 expedition down the Mississippi River reported that the Koroas decorated their houses with "great round plates of shining copper, made like pot covers." Outdoor cooking fires and above-ground granaries were also constructed near each house. Houses were arranged around an open central plaza with a temple at one end. Some French observers witnessed Tunica temples built on artificial, flat-topped mounds.

Corn and squashes were important food staples. Unlike many Southeastern Indians, Tunica men—not women—were responsible for agricultural activities. Wild plant foods were also collected, including persimmons and other fruits, berries, nuts, seeds, roots, and herbs. Deer, bear, and occasionally buffalo were hunted. Like the

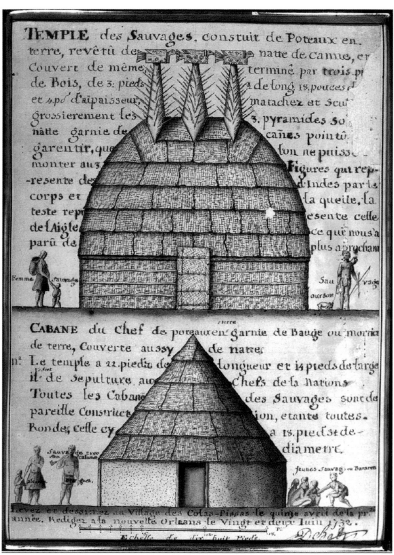

"Temple des Sauvages, Cabane du Chef," pen and ink by Alexandre de Batz, New Orleans, 1732 (courtesy of the Peabody Museum, Harvard University, N19413, photograph by Hillel Burger)

Caddo, Tunicas produced salt at seeps and other natural deposits, some of which they traded to other groups.

Tunica men wore deerskin loincloths during the warm seasons and decorated themselves with tattoos, beads, and pendants. Women wore short fringed skirts of cloth made from the inner bark of mulberry trees. Women also tattooed themselves and further enhanced their appearance with beads, pendants, and earrings. They kept their hair in a single long braid that hung down the back or was wrapped about the crown. In cold weather, men and women wore mantles of mulberry bark cloth, turkey feathers, or muskrat skins.

According to early French accounts, Tunica Indians were only minimally involved in the deerskin trade—an important Indian and European exchange system promoted mainly by the British throughout much of the South. This was perhaps due in part to the Tunica's disinclination toward any sort of interaction with British colonists. Indeed, pressures felt by the Tunicas stemming from the expanding influence of English traders and their native allies on the eastern side of the Mississippi led them to abandon their settlements along the lower Yazoo River in 1706. Moving farther down the Mississippi, the Tunicas established a handful of new villages at a location across from the mouth of the Red River known as Portage de la Croix.

Their new location put the Tunicas close to colonial French settlements. Inveterate traders, the Tunicas were by this time becoming ever more dependent upon European goods; however, they continued to arrange their villages according to traditional patterns and to manufacture many of their own goods, including shell-tempered pottery. Although the Tunicas made a pretense of accepting the teachings of French missionaries, the persistence of traditional ceremonies and burial practices suggests that their own religious beliefs remained vibrant.

Throughout the eighteenth century, the Tunica-French alliance worked well for both groups: the Tunicas supplied the French with food and horses in exchange for European manufactured goods. Tunica warriors also provided military assistance to the French,

SAUVAGE matachez en Guerrier, ayant fait trois Chevelu
cest a dire ayant tuez trois Hommes Natchez.
A. Bride les Bœufs Chef des Thonicas, il remply la place de
son predecesseur que les natchez Tuerrent au mois de juin
dernier. B. Femme chef Veufue du — defunt E. Iacob. fils
du deffunt H. cheuelures matachéeuer le baton pareilleme
desinez d'apres nature Sur les — lieux,
Redigez à la n.ᵘᵉ Orleans le 22. Iuin 1732.

"Buffalo Tamer, Chief of the Tunicas" by Alexandre de Batz,
New Orleans, 1732 (courtesy of the Peabody Museum, Harvard
University, N19413, photograph by Hillel Burger)

61

"Sauvage a la chasse," by François Dumont de Montigny
(courtesy of the Newberry Library, Chicago)

which sometimes brought retribution from other Indian groups. For example, in 1730 the Tunicas assisted the French in an attack on the Natchez Indians, in retaliation for their uprising the previous year in which nearly 700 French soldiers and settlers in the colony surrounding Fort Rosalie (at present-day Natchez, Mississippi) were killed. In 1731 the Natchez took revenge upon the Tunicas, killing their chief and many warriors. In the battle that followed, the Tunica settlements at Portage de la Croix were devastated.

Moving a few miles farther down the Mississippi River, but remaining on the eastern side, the Tunicas reestablished themselves in 1731 at a place that came to be known as Tunica Bayou. Now a single settlement sufficed to shelter the Tunica's dwindling population, although once again the traditional village layout was used. The cemetery associated with this settlement produced the fabulous

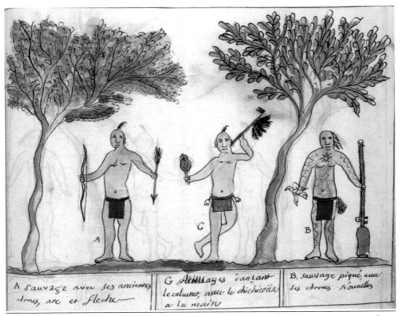

"Three Indians," by François Dumont de Montigny (courtesy of the Newberry Library, Chicago)

"Tunica Treasure"—the burial goods, both aboriginal and European, unearthed in the 1960s by a grave robber and subsequently returned to the Tunica-Biloxi tribe under a federal court ruling. They are now on exhibit in the tribal museum at Marksville. This collection is noteworthy in that it demonstrates not only the vast amount of trade goods the Tunicas were able to acquire from the French, but also the persistence of traditional craftwork, social organization, and burial practices.

With the English acquisition in 1763 of lands on the eastern side of the Mississippi River, the Tunicas moved a few more miles downstream to a site directly across from the French settlement at Point Coupee. There they were able to maintain peace with the English while continuing their active trading relations with the French. When Spain extended its domination over all of Louisiana in 1781, the Tunicas accepted an alliance with the colonial government. Despite generally positive relations this alliance created, the influx of white settlers along the Mississippi forced the Tunicas to relocate once again, this time several miles up the Red River to an area near present-day Marksville, Louisiana. There the Tunicas were well positioned to continue their involvement in trade with Europeans as well as with other Indians, though now the direction of their trade turned increasingly towards the west. Agricultural activities declined during this period, although the Tunicas were able to make good use of the rich natural resources of their new land. In the following decades the Tunicas absorbed the remnants of even less fortunate tribes such as the Avoyel, Biloxi, Choctaw, and Ofo.

4

CHANGES:
Nineteenth and Twentieth
Century Developments

Two major developments of the nineteenth and twentieth centuries had a profound impact on American Indians. First, many groups, including those living in and around Arkansas, lost their original homelands. These losses were sometimes the result of military defeat, but more often they were a consequence of treaties signed with federal or state governments in which Indians ceded their homelands in exchange for reserved lands in Indian Territory and promises of assistance that only rarely were kept. The second development involved pressures put on relocated Indians to abandon traditional beliefs and practices and adopt the more "civilized" life of white rural American society. Federal government policies toward Indians during much of the nineteenth and early twentieth centuries, along with many corresponding laws, were based on the "melting pot" theory, which promoted the idea that American society would be better off if everyone were alike. These policies and laws conspired to eradicate American Indian cultures.

Under these pressures—which included laws forbidding such aspects of American Indian culture as native marriage and child rearing practices, religion, ceremony, dress, art, and even language—

many traditional beliefs and practices were abandoned while others were secretly retained. The most cherished aspects of traditional culture, carefully hidden from open display, proved to be remarkably resilient and were periodically resurrected and expressed in the context of native revitalization movements. Revitalization movements are crusades that lead to a reformulation of traditional cultural patterns, often with the addition of new religious beliefs and practices, in order to "revitalize" communities that have suffered oppression at the hands of a domineering society.

One such movement was the Ghost Dance, which consisted of a set of rituals and associated beliefs combining traditional American Indian themes with several elements of Christianity. Many Indian groups adopted the Ghost Dance in the late nineteenth century in the hope that it would bring back the happiness and harmony said to have existed before contact with whites. The Ghost Dance, like many other revitalization movements, provoked swift and harsh responses from the federal government. At Wounded Knee, South Dakota, in 1890, more than 250 Lakota Sioux men, women, and children were slaughtered by the U.S. Army following the performance of a Ghost Dance.

In the twentieth century, federal government policy shifted first to benign neglect of Indians, then to support of Indian freedom of cultural expression. These shifts brought forth a resurgence of indigenous beliefs and practices, many of them now interwoven with various threads of white American culture. That these traditional beliefs and practices survived more than four centuries of persistent efforts to eradicate them by successive Spanish, French, and American governments is clear testimony to the tremendous depth and resilience of American Indian cultures.

The Quapaws

The Quapaws were steadfast allies of both French and Spanish colonists in Louisiana Territory in the seventeenth and eighteenth centuries. They benefited from their alliances with colonial agents mainly through the development of trade relations. Although they readily accepted missionaries, they were less interested in reorganiz-

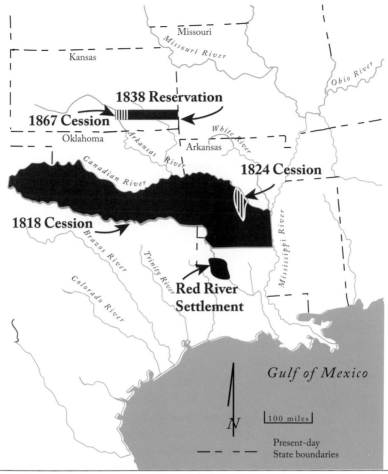

locations of the Quapaw Indians in the nineteenth century

ing their lives according to the tenets of Catholicism than they were in converting the presence of missionaries in their villages into yet another mechanism for solidifying relations with European allies. To advance these relations, Quapaws allowed French and Spanish traders, settlers, and military personnel to occupy lands in the vicinity of Arkansas Post (the location of which changed several times during the colonial era). The main benefit the Europeans derived from this alliance was not economic, but military: colonial governors found that they could nearly always rely on the Quapaws for assistance in campaigns against rival Indian groups in the Mississippi Valley who were allied with the British.

After 1803 representatives of the United States replaced the Spaniards stationed at Arkansas Post. The Quapaws attempted to maintain the same kind of relationship they had had with European colonial regimes, but while the Americans professed interest in continuing these relations, the demands they placed upon the Quapaws were much different from the requests for military assistance that the French and Spanish had been making for more than a century. What the Americans wanted was land—first for the purpose of relocating dispossessed Indians from east of the Mississippi River and later to serve as a frontier zone for expanding non-Indian settlement.

In 1818 the Quapaws signed a treaty with the United States ceding more than 43 million acres of lands they claimed south of the Arkansas River, reserving for themselves a comparatively small tract of approximately one million acres south of the Arkansas River southeast of Little Rock. The ceded lands would provide ample territory—so thought the government—for immigrant tribes who would be resettled from homelands east of the Mississippi. The Quapaws were given $4000 worth of manufactured goods in payment for the ceded land, and then were promised annual payments of additional goods valued at $1000. Perhaps of greater value to the Quapaws was the formal recognition they received for signing the treaty and the corresponding expectation that they would be consulted on future matters concerning U.S. Indian policy west of the Mississippi River.

The relationship established by the treaty, if adhered to, would have preserved the pattern of mutual respect and obligation the Quapaws had maintained in their alliances with French and Spanish colonial governments, but the U.S. government had different ideas about dealing with Indian tribes. It failed to pay the first annuity. The Quapaws also began to suffer from increasingly frequent attacks by the Osages, who had ceded their Arkansas lands in 1808, and from encroachments upon their territory by other Indians and by non-Indian settlers. As a result, the Quapaws became destitute. In response to repeated pleas for assistance under the provisions of the 1818 treaty, the government eventually offered to purchase the Quapaws' remaining lands in Arkansas (to make way for non-Indian settlement). The Indians would be relocated to lands along the Red River in Louisiana adjacent to the Caddo Indians. They would also receive supplies and assistance to reestablish their villages in the new location. The Quapaws initially rejected this offer, but in the end realized they had no other choice. In 1824 they signed a second treaty with the United States, and their move to the Red River took place in 1826. Antoine Barraque, a French trader with experience among the Quapaws, led 455 men, women, and children to the Red River in January and February of that year.

Although the Caddos did nothing directly to challenge the Quapaw resettlement, they generally treated the newcomers as unwelcome guests. Even less kind was nature itself: the Quapaws first planting of crops was destroyed by Red River floods in the spring of 1826. A second planting was also lost to floods. With all the supplies the government had provided gone, starvation gripped the Quapaws and many died. At that point, for the first time in their history, the Quapaws divided into two factions. One faction was led by Sarasin, a chief of mixed French-Quapaw descent. This group, about one-fourth of the population, returned to the ancestral homelands along the Arkansas River. They were able to settle on lands that had been granted to about a dozen Quapaws with partial French ancestry, but in doing so they relinquished claims to the annuities they were allowed under the provisions of the 1824 treaty. The other group, led by Heckaton, a full-blood chief, was determined to persevere in the Red River settlement. Though additional government assistance was obtained, Red River floods continued to destroy Quapaw crops. Gradually, over the next few years, virtually all of Heckaton's group returned to the Arkansas River.

In 1830 Chief Heckaton traveled to Washington to report the desperate poverty of his people. This time the government responded with an offer to remove the Quapaws from Arkansas to reservation lands in the newly established Indian Territory. Reluctant at first to give up completely and finally the lands in which their ancestors were buried, the Quapaws saw that, once again, they had no choice but to go along with the government's wishes. In 1833 a third treaty was signed that provided the Quapaws with 150 square miles of land in northeastern Indian Territory. They were also promised agricultural equipment, a blacksmith, and a farmer to help get them started on their new lands, and an annuity of $2000. An additional $1000 per year would be furnished for educational purposes.

As a result of these treaties, the Quapaws lost their aboriginal homelands in Arkansas and remained divided into two factions, each with different views on what to do about their loss of lands and livelihood. These developments, along with additional population losses from starvation and disease, continued to erode traditional patterns of social and political organization. Despite everything, the Quapaws maintained a strong sense of identity with their past, and their status as a formally recognized tribe was preserved in the various treaties they signed with the United States.

Before the U.S. Senate ratified the treaty of 1833, the leadership contest between Sarasin and Heckaton intensified to the point where Sarasin led his group, now numbering about 300, back to the Red River. In 1834 Heckaton led his 161 followers to the newly granted lands in Indian Territory. This group was guided by federal Indian agent Wharton Rector to a location along the Neosho River, and improvements to the land were immediately begun. Two years later it was discovered that Rector had led the Quapaws to the wrong location. Once again they were forced to vacate their homes, this time without any compensation for the improvements they had made or for the loss of their crops.

Some Quapaws now deserted Heckaton's band and joined Sarasin's group, which by this time had left the Red River and joined a group of Creek Indians living on the north side of the Canadian River in east-central Oklahoma. The combined Creek-Quapaw community attempted to maintain a traditional Southeastern

Indian lifestyle. Meanwhile, the reservation Quapaws remaining with Heckaton began again the arduous task of establishing a new agricultural settlement. This group was forced by the provisions of their agreement with the U.S. government to give up the traditional village-based settlement pattern and communal economic organization, and adopt the white American pattern of living on individual, economically independent farmsteads.

Despite the split between Sarasin's and Heckaton's factions, the Quapaws were able to maintain some measure of tribal solidarity. Twice a year they came together as a single tribe: when annuities were disbursed at the reservation, and when the summer Green Corn ceremony was held. These get-togethers enabled the Quapaws to preserve many traditional elements of social organization and keep alive many of their religious beliefs.

The maintenance of cultural traditions did not sit well with the U.S. government, whose aim at that time was to eradicate all vestiges of "Indianness" among its dependent tribes and blend them into rural white American society. One government strategy in support of this aim was to require the education of Indian youths, preferably at schools located away from the reservation where students would not be influenced by traditional values. The Quapaws convinced a Methodist minister, Samuel G. Patterson, to set up a school near their reservation in 1843 and for a while this kept Quapaw youngsters at home. But when the Methodist school was closed a decade later, the Quapaws had to send their children to a Catholic school in Kansas.

Tribal factionalism took a new turn during the Civil War. The reservation Quapaws sided with the Confederacy, while the Canadian River group joined a pro-Union organization composed of representatives of various Indian tribes. As was generally the case, both groups suffered tremendously during this conflict and many families were forced to flee their homes. At the end of the war, some Quapaws returned to the reservation, but many, including Tallchief, the last hereditary leader, joined the Osages who were living on a large reservation farther west in Indian Territory. The

Osages invited the Quapaws to join them in a confederacy, but the transplanted Quapaws ultimately declined.

In an effort to make the best use of their meager land base, and lacking the tools and labor necessary to survive on farming alone, several Quapaws in the final quarter of the nineteenth century chose to rent some of their property to non-Indian farmers in exchange for one-third of the harvest, while others began to collect fees from Texas cattlemen who annually crossed Quapaw lands with herds enroute to Kansas railheads. But the federal government's view concerning the assimilation of Indians into rural white American society was based on the assumption that the Indians would be farmers, not commodity brokers or land barons, so these entrepreneurial activities were quickly brought to an end.

By the end of the nineteenth century, few Quapaws remained on the reservation. This posed a serious threat, because their legal title to the reservation was valid only "as long as they shall exist as a nation or continue to reside thereon." With the assistance of a transplanted New York Stockbridge Indian, A. W. Abrams, who had been adopted into the Quapaw tribe, the reservation group succeeded in enlarging the tribal roll (the official membership list submitted to the federal government) by getting Quapaws living with the Osages to enlist, by encouraging Quapaws still living in Arkansas to move to the reservation, and finally by adopting into the tribe a number of other displaced or "homeless" Indians.

This expansion of the tribal roll was accomplished none too soon, for in 1887 Congress passed the Indian Allotment Act, or Dawes Act, which required reservations to be split up into individual family allotments. Any "surplus" or unallotted lands could then be sold to non-Indians. Although the Dawes Act stipulated 160-acre allotments for every adult, the Quapaws fought for and won the authority to assign 200-acre allotments. Most of the Quapaw lands were allotted in contiguous parcels, so even with the official abolition of Indian Territory and dismantling of the reservation system after the turn of the century, the Quapaws preserved a large and valuable land base.

With the allotment of tribal lands, 40 acres were set aside on which St. Mary's of the Quapaws, a Catholic-run school, was established. For nearly three decades this school was supported in part by a $1000 educational annuity the tribe received from the federal government.

At the turn of the twentieth century, zinc and lead deposits were discovered in contiguous portions of Kansas and Oklahoma that included lands owned by Quapaws. Leases to mine operators brought much money into Quapaw hands, but with this windfall came other, less fortunate, consequences. The Quapaws wanted to manage their assets without government intervention. In keeping with a shift in U.S. policy towards relinquishing administrative control of Indian affairs, the government gave nominal consent to the Quapaws' plans for economic development. But ceaseless incidents of corrupt business practices by unscrupulous mining speculators and operators, many involving the swindling of elderly Quapaws out of substantial fortunes, soon forced the government to take action aimed at regulating the mining industry. The result was that the Quapaws continued to be dependent wards of the U.S. government.

One positive effect of government intervention during the early decades of the twentieth century was that Quapaws did receive most of the revenue from leased mineral rights. But this wealth was distributed unevenly among tribal members, most of it going to individuals who owned large tracts in the western part of the Quapaw lands. It so happened that these individuals were mainly full-bloods, who were outnumbered on the tribal roll by Quapaws of mixed descent, some of whom still lived with the Osages. The old factionalism from the days of Sarasin and Heckaton gave way to a new split between a small group of wealthy full-bloods and a larger group of poor mixed-bloods.

This division affected other aspects of twentieth century Quapaw tribal affairs. Toward the end of the nineteenth century, the Quapaws took up the peyote religion, a widespread revitalization movement that combined elements of traditional religious beliefs,

Christianity, and the use of peyote as a sacrament and as a means to acquire power. The peyote religion was introduced to the Quapaws by John "Moonhead" Wilson, of mixed French-Caddo-Delaware descent, who had witnessed peyote use among Comanche Indians. Wilson developed a version of the religion organized around his Big Moon Peyote Altar, which embodied symbols of Jesus Christ and other themes that appealed to the predominantly Catholic Quapaws.

The affluent full-bloods were the most ardent proponents of Wilson's brand of peyote religion, while the less well-to-do mixed-bloods sustained more traditional religious beliefs. Traditional beliefs and practices associated with naming children and mourning and burying the dead were maintained among both groups. Wealthy full-bloods also fostered community spirit by distributing gifts among their tribesmen at powwows and at other times. Although the peyote religion fostered a broader "Indian" identity among its participants, it displaced many traditional religious beliefs.

The social division by wealth also played a role in the organization and actions of the Quapaw Tribal Council, the governing body created as a result of the Indian Allotment Act. The affluent full-bloods transferred some of the personal responsibility ethic emphasized in their newly adopted religious practices to the economic and political matters that were the primary business of the Tribal Council, which they controlled. Under their influence the Tribal Council in 1927 terminated support for St. Mary's School. They also rejected the Bureau of Indian Affairs program, advanced under the Indian Reorganization Act of 1934, which advocated self-determination among American Indians and encouraged a return to communally based tribal endeavors.

Full-blood Quapaws retained their language and traditional dress longer than the mixed-bloods; in fact, a few Quapaws are still able to speak the language. Participation in the peyote religion through the Native American Church helped to maintain an "Indian" identity within the wider American society. Throughout the twentieth century, other social and ceremonial events, especially the annual powwow, have played a central role in sustaining a strong sense of cultural heritage among the Quapaws.

In 1956 the Tribal Council was replaced by a Quapaw Business Committee consisting of an elected chairman, a vice-chairman, a secretary-treasurer, and four council members. The Business Committee is responsible for oversight of tribal affairs including economic enterprises, land and lease management, administration of federal programs formerly run by the Bureau of Indian Affairs, and administration of social service and educational programs.

While this decision-making body is the culmination of the changes in economy, politics, social organization, and governance that have taken place since the beginning of the colonial era, its actions have fostered a contemporary revitalization of traditional values among the Quapaw people. For example, a federal judgment in 1951 concerning claims made under the 1824 treaty awarded the Quapaws nearly $1,000,000. The distribution of this sum in 1961 to 1199 Quapaws identified on the tribal roll did not turn anyone into an instant millionaire, but it did stimulate interaction among a large number of people, many of whom had been long separated from their traditional cultural heritage, thus increasing the number of Quapaws carrying their Indian identity into the future.

The Osages

Europeans contacted the Osages later than other Indians in and around Arkansas. By the time regular interaction began in the eighteenth century, French trading operations were well developed in the Louisiana Territory, with major market centers at St. Louis and New Orleans. With their villages located along the Missouri and Osage rivers, the Osages occupied a strategic position between the Mississippi Valley and the Great Plains. They quickly became middlemen in the French and later the Spanish fur trade, channeling furs, horses, and various other commodities from west to east.

With the acquisition of guns and horses at the beginning of the eighteenth century, the Osages became economically dependent upon Europeans. The benefits they received from this dependency were not limited to material goods. With their guns and horses, the Osages were able to expand their territory, often at the expense of other Indian tribes, taking control of large portions of Missouri, Arkansas, Oklahoma, and Kansas. Much diplomatic effort was required on the part of French and Spanish colonial officials to halt the juggernaut of Osage expansionism when, by the late eighteenth century, they were raiding deep into Texas and Louisiana.

The successes the Osages enjoyed during the era of European colonialism were not to continue into the American period. At the beginning of the nineteenth century, a primary concern of the American government was to develop the frontier by establishing permanent industrial and agricultural settlements throughout the entire region east of the Mississippi. This meant there would be no room for Indians (who still were regarded as free-wandering savages, even though most were in fact settled farmers), or for frontier huntsmen of any race. Eastern Indians and frontiersmen alike were pressured to move westward to, among other places, the lands controlled by the Osages.

As immigrant Indians moved west of the Mississippi, many joined forces with the Osages' traditional foes, including the Potawatomis, Sacs, and Foxes to the north, and the Quapaws and Caddos to the south. During the early years following the Louisiana Purchase, a tremendous amount of warfare spread across the southern frontier as the Osages sought to protect their domain. In response to these conditions, the U.S. government sought major land cessions which they eventually obtained in treaties of 1808, 1818, and 1825. As a condition of the 1808 treaty, the Osages ceded lands comprising virtually all of northern Arkansas. In exchange for these cessions, they were granted a sizable reservation in south-central Kansas in 1825.

Initially the Osages were able to maintain their traditional lifeways on the reservation. One significant modification of seasonal activities, however, was a greater emphasis on the summer buffalo hunt. When the buffalo were nearly exterminated in the last quarter of the nineteenth century, the Osages suffered. With the rapidly growing pressure for additional lands for non-Indian settlement on the Plains, and with the Osages increasingly viewed as "worthless

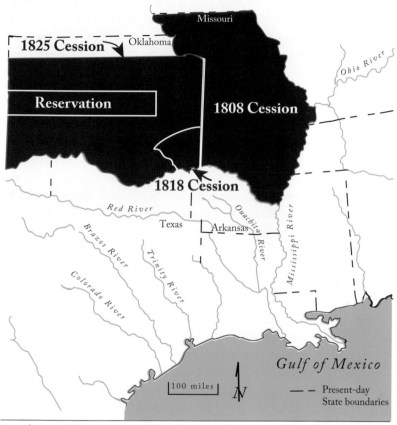

locations of the Osage Indians in the nineteenth century

vagabonds," the federal government in 1865 arranged for the sale of their lands in Kansas and moved them to a new reservation in Indian Territory. Here, a split developed between the mixed-bloods, who settled together in one area, and the full-bloods, who divided themselves into a number of communities reflecting traditional band divisions. This split widened when other Indians, including the Quapaws, joined the Osages.

Unable to hunt and generally unsuccessful in their attempts to adopt a settled agrarian life, many Osages became dependent on federal Indian agents for support. As annuities accumulated from the sale of their Kansas lands, a substantial monetary fund was created. This enabled the full-blood communities to maintain many of their cultural traditions. In contrast, most of the mixed-bloods opted for pursuit of a rural agrarian life that differed little from that of their white neighbors.

In 1881 the Osage National Council was created with much encouragement from the U.S. government. This was supported by full-bloods as well as by mixed-bloods, perhaps because by this time traditional political institutions had largely collapsed. Moreover, in subsequent years the number of full-bloods declined, while the number of mixed-bloods increased. By the beginning of the twentieth century, mixed bloods were in the majority. At the same time the federal government decided to abolish the Osage National Council and replace it with a Business Committee, organized in 1904.

The Business Committee, under the control of the mixed-bloods, voted in favor of allotment of reservation lands to some 2229 persons then on the tribal roll. Providentially, the Business Committee retained tribal control of mineral rights on allotted lands, and no surplus lands were set aside for sale to non-Indians. Therefore, when a demand arose during World War I for tapping oil deposits below their lands, the Osage tribe became extraordinarily wealthy. While many of the full-bloods chose to remain close to traditional lifestyles (albeit supplemented by ownership of expensive automobiles and other luxuries), the economic security provided by the oil boom propelled a large number of the mixed-bloods squarely into mainstream white society.

As the number of full-bloods continued to decline, it became increasingly difficult to maintain several key features of traditional social and political organization. Clan organization broke down, and the various levels of civil and ceremonial leadership associated with the clan organization ceased to function. Several late nineteenth century religious developments laid a foundation for subsequent revitalization movements among twentieth century Osages. In 1884 they acquired the iloshka dance from Kansa Indians. The iloshka dance centers on the ceremonial selection of a young boy to serve as tribal drumkeeper and involves several days of gift giving, feasting, dancing, and visiting coordinated among participating villages. The Ghost Dance was introduced in 1891-92 by John Wilson , a member of the Red River Delaware-Caddo community, though it failed to generate much interest. In 1897 John Wilson also brought his Big Moon peyote religion to the Osage. These ceremonies served to fill the void left by the erosion of traditional social arrangements and associated religious beliefs.

During the initial decades of the twentieth century, peyotism became the dominant religious practice. Part of its attraction was the emphasis placed on accommodation with white American society, a theme that resonated positively throughout the largely mixed-blood Osage community. The dominance of peyote religion became so great that most of the religious elements of the iloshka ceremony were eliminated, and it became mainly a social ceremony.

The Depression years brought to a close the era of fabulous wealth among the Osages, but by this time most people on the tribal roll had become full-time participants in white American society. For this reason, the efforts of the Bureau of Indian Affairs to implement the provisions of the Indian Reorganization Act gained little headway among the Osages, the majority of whom saw little purpose in a return to traditional patterns of consensual government. Descendants of the full-bloods, however, maintained a separate "Indian community" in northeastern Oklahoma, where attempts to combine acceptance of contemporary economic realities with the celebration of culturally distinctive values and beliefs continue to the present.

The Caddo Indians

Occupying a large region separating the northeastern frontier of New Spain and the southwestern frontier of the Louisiana territory, the Caddo Indians played a crucial role in the contests for empire that developed among European colonial powers in southern North America. During the seventeenth and eighteenth centuries the Spaniards hoped to "civilize" the settled agrarian Caddos and convert them to Christianity. The Caddos, however, were uninterested in congregating their dispersed settlements into mission communities. Their allegiance to their own ancient and well-ordered patterns of social organization, community leadership, and religious beliefs doomed the periodic attempts of small numbers of Spanish priests and soldiers to bring the Caddos within the Spanish colonial system. But the French colonial government, by merely permitting traders to operate among the Caddos, succeeded in reducing them to economic dependency within only a few decades.

By the late eighteenth century, both Spanish and French colonial governments were troubled by the fact that their adjacent frontier zones were becoming theaters of increasing warfare among numerous Indian groups. In their attempts to bring peace to these regions, the Europeans found the Caddos to be valuable intermediaries. A number of Caddo "medal chiefs" (leaders who were presented with large commemorative medals, usually decorated with the image of the reigning French or Spanish monarch) seemed to be particularly successful in bringing together representatives of warring Indian tribes and hammering out peace treaties among them. This facility in international diplomacy was no doubt the product of the Caddos' highly structured leadership institutions, coupled with their long history of arranging alliances among their own confederates, as well as with other tribes, for purposes of trade, defense, and other matters of mutual concern.

When the United States inherited control of the Louisiana Territory after 1803, it too found the Caddo Indians to be valuable allies. One of the first things the Americans decided was that the vast newly acquired territory needed to be explored and mapped. The Caddo Indians assisted William Dunbar and Dr. George Hunter in exploring the Ouachita River in 1804, and Colonel Thomas Freeman and Dr. Peter Custis in exploring the Red River in 1805. In 1807 Caddo leaders at Natchitoches organized a large intertribal council for U.S. agent John Sibley. It was attended by representatives of various Caddo groups, along with Comanches, Tawakonis, Kichais, and Chickasaws. At this council Sibley and

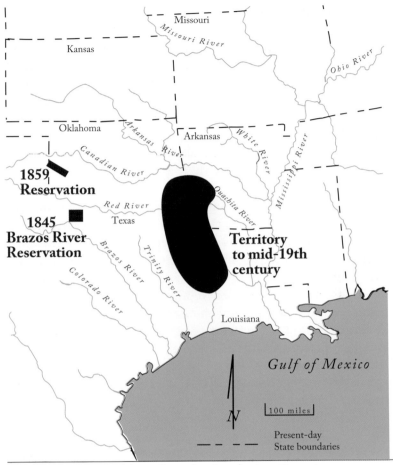

Locations of the Caddo Indians in the nineteenth century

Colonel Zebulon Pike signed a peace treaty between the United States and the attending tribes and won promises that troubles between the Caddos and immigrant Choctaws would be brought to an end.

While the Caddos remained numerous and powerful throughout most of their aboriginal territory at the beginning of the American era, they too were affected by disease, depredations at the hands of enemy tribes, shifting balances among colonial powers, and the encroachment of increasing numbers of immigrant Indian and non-Indian settlers. These circumstances brought about the collapse of some of the earlier alliances, including those of the Natchitoches and Kadohadacho. Members of these formerly powerful alliances joined together in the latter decades of the eighteenth century and moved from their aboriginal homelands to a new location along the Red River close to the Mississippi, settling along Sodo Bayou, which later was renamed Caddo Bayou.

As some Caddos vacated their aboriginal homelands, other eastern tribes began to move into the region. Among these early nineteenth century immigrants were Cherokees, Choctaws, Delawares, Koasatis (also known as Coushattas), Alabamas, and Shawnees. Osage Indians from southwest Missouri continued to raid deep into Caddo territory in Arkansas and Texas. Comanches, Apaches, and other Southern Plains tribes attacked from the west. Non-Indian settlers also began to infiltrate the region, causing additional hardships for Caddos and immigrant tribes alike.

In response, the Caddos and some of the immigrant tribes developed alliances for aid and defense of the lands they had settled. For example, in 1804 the Caddos permitted Koasatis and Alabamas to settle among them, and in 1817 Cherokees and Delawares were allowed to establish villages along the Red River. Later the Choctaws were permitted to join the growing alliance that the Caddo leaders were organizing. This alliance established a defensive perimeter of villages that provided protection from the Osages. But Caddo leaders were selective in cementing diplomatic relations intended to enhance the security of Indian settlements. For example, the immigration of some Indians in the region, including the Quapaws, was resisted. Even so, American authorities were able to rely on the neutrality of allied tribes under Caddoan leadership during both the War of 1812 and the Mexican War of Independence, in return for which some measure of protection was provided from illegal settlement by non-Indians on Caddo lands.

Many Caddo Indians nonetheless fell prey to the continuing efforts of non-Indians to displace them. Pressures built from in-

"Long Hat's Camp, a Caddo farmstead in eastern Oklahoma, 1868-1872," photograph by William S. Soule (courtesy of the Smithsonian Institution)

creasing settlement of whites along the Red River, and attempts by the newly organized Mexican government in the early nineteenth century to encourage the Louisiana Caddos to join their kinsmen in Texas. Thus, when the United States offered in 1835 to purchase Caddo lands in Louisiana for $80,000—also exacting the Caddos' promise never to return to American territory—these already-displaced Indians jumped at the opportunity.

Unfortunately, the Texas revolution for independence from Mexico broke out in October of that year, putting the Louisiana Caddos in limbo for the next few years. Eventually they did move, but the newly organized Republic of Texas considered them intruders and pressured the United States to take them back. Unsuccessful in this effort, the Texas government eventually reached an accord with the Indians, but over the next several years severe animosities developed between Indians and non-Indian settlers in northeastern Texas. Acts of violence were frequent. Hostilities were ended during the early 1840s by another series of treaties arranged with the Caddos by President Sam Houston of the Republic of Texas.

When Texas became a state in 1845, the Caddos were given lands along the Brazos River. Here they endured a series of crop failures, were forced to compete with other Indian and non-Indian settlers for scarce game, and suffered continuing depredations by malevolent whites. A United States military officer visiting the region in 1851 noted that the Caddos had been reduced to a "starving condition."

Fortunately for the Caddos, the federal agent responsible for many of the Texas tribes, Robert S. Neighbors, was committed to the idea of restoring some measure of dignity to the lives of these people. He arranged their relocation in 1859 to newly reserved lands in Indian Territory. When the move was completed, Neighbors wrote "I have this day crossed all of the Indians out of the heathen land of 'Texas' and am now out of the land of the Philistines." The Texans lost no love on Neighbors, either: he returned the following year only to be shot in the back and killed. He is buried in a cemetery at Fort Belknap, where the Caddo Indians still pay their respects to his grave.

On their new lands, the Caddos set about reestablishing their farming communities along traditional lines of social and political organization. Old alignments were reinstituted insofar as they could be. Each community appointed its own caddi, who was assisted by a council of elders, or canahas. Community activities were organized by the town tanmas. Although their lives were disrupted by the Civil War, the Caddos were again able to develop the mechanisms necessary to maintain a traditionally ordered community.

But the passage of the Dawes Act in 1887 brought an end to these efforts to preserve traditional lifeways. Reserved lands were allotted in 1902 and the reservation ceased to exist. Large tracts of "surplus land" were taken by the federal government and eventually sold to non-Indian settlers. Government efforts were aimed at destroying Indian culture by banning native language, political organization, religious beliefs, marriage and family practices, and even dress and art. The Caddos and many other Indian groups were forced to take traditional beliefs, values, and practices "underground" or at least keep them safely indoors. In the 1890s Caddos adopted the Ghost Dance and were introduced to the peyote religion by Arapaho Indians. These religious movements represent the first steps taken along a path of revitalization that extends to the present.

Some relief from the oppressive consequences of the Dawes Act was afforded by passage of the Indian Reorganization Act of 1934, which reversed earlier government objectives to eradicate American Indian cultures. Thus, it was possible for the Caddos in 1938 to organize their own governing Tribal Council, whose decision-making responsibilities were guided by a formally adopted constitution. The chairman and council members (including a vice-chairman, secretary-treasurer, and two councilmen) were empowered to promote tribal welfare through development of tribal resources, acquisition of new lands, preservation of existing landholdings, and promotion of improved land use. A credit program and other services were developed to support these endeavors.

Although the formation of the Tribal Council did much to promote self-determination among Caddo Indians, gains in welfare were not accomplished without some additional problems. One such problem was confusion over the roles of the Tribal Council, headed by the elected chairman (or nit-tso-sah-dos-cha-ah, "one who takes the chair"), and the traditional leaders, headed by the caddi. The confusion arose partly due to the fact that for many years both positions were occupied by the same man and there were no conflicting interests. Beginning in the 1970s, however, these positions were occupied by different men, making more obvious the distinction between traditional and nontraditional forms of government. This distinction was further underscored when women began to be elected to these positions, formerly held only by men.

Cherokee Immigrants in Arkansas

In the second half of the eighteenth century, small numbers of Cherokees began to spend winters hunting in the valleys of the St. Francis, White, and Arkansas rivers in Spanish Louisiana. Toward the end of the century, some Cherokee groups petitioned the Spanish government for rights to settle permanently on these lands. Although the Osages and Quapaws resisted these petitions,

Spanish officials consented. By the turn of the nineteenth century, more than a thousand Cherokees had been permitted to settle along the St. Francis River.

Following the Louisiana Purchase in 1803, the Jefferson administration continued to encourage Eastern Cherokees (most of whom lived in Tennessee, North and South Carolina, and Georgia) to emigrate to Arkansas, and settlements began to grow along the Arkansas River. With the land cession obtained by the federal government from the Osages in 1808, vast tracts of land north of the Arkansas River were opened for immigrant tribes. Between 1809 and 1812 approximately 2000 Cherokees settled along the White and St. Francis rivers and in the Arkansas River Valley upstream from Little Rock. In 1817 the Arkansas (or Western) Cherokees signed a treaty with the United States by which they obtained a large reservation in north-central Arkansas between the Arkansas and White rivers, encompassing most of the northwest quarter of the state.

The Cherokees brought to Arkansas a lifeway that differed substantially from those of the neighboring Quapaws and Osages. During the seventeenth and eighteenth centuries, the Eastern Cherokees had been in close contact with British and American colonists. As a result, their culture had undergone tremendous change. The Eastern Cherokees adopted the agriculturally based subsistence economy of the Europeans, complete with animal husbandry and plow agriculture. They also accepted many European beliefs and values. Early travelers in Arkansas often described Cherokee settlements as differing little from nearby white settlements. Cherokee houses, dress, and daily activity patterns all blended well into frontier Arkansas society.

There were, however, some features that served to distinguish the Arkansas Cherokees from other groups. One was a pattern of village organization in which charismatic leaders employed social and political skills on behalf of their communities. Many of these leaders, including Duwali (often called The Bowl), Takatoka, and

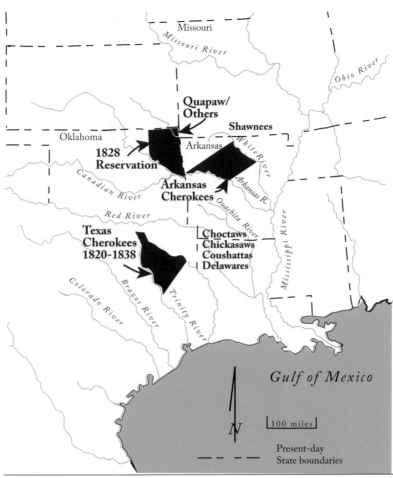

Locations of the Cherokee and other immigrants in the nineteenth century

Tolontuskee, had been leaders of Eastern Cherokee settlements until factionalism brought them and their followers to Arkansas. Tolontuskee, who became the leader of a large community scattered along Illinois Bayou a few miles upstream from the Arkansas River, rose to a position of prominence among the entire Arkansas Cherokee population. Proclaiming the occupied portion of the Arkansas Valley "the promised land for the Cherokee future," his diplomatic activities were instrumental in bringing about the 1817 treaty. In 1818 he petitioned the American Board of Commissioners for Foreign Missions to establish a mission among the Arkansas Cherokees. This request brought Cephus Washburn and Albert Finney to Arkansas in 1820, the year after Tolontuskee died. Tolontuskee was succeeded by his brother, John Jolly, a strong advocate of educational programs. With Jolly's support, Dwight Mission was built along Illinois Bayou in the vicinity of Tolontuskee's settlement. It served the Arkansas Cherokees both as a mission and as a school for children until their removal to Indian Territory in 1828.

A second distinctive feature of Cherokee culture in Arkansas was the periodic gathering of people for the performance of ceremonies, including the traditional Green Corn ceremony. These ceremonies were typically held at special grounds located in or adjacent to each community. They served to reinforce the solidarity of village residents, many of whom lived miles apart in scattered farmsteads, and to keep alive many traditional beliefs about the sacred relationships between the Cherokees and the social and natural worlds in which they lived.

The Cherokees were successful in adapting their agrarian communities to the new Arkansas lands. One famous resident was Sequoyah, the brilliant inventor of the Cherokee alphabet. (While he lived in Arkansas, he worked as a saltmaker.) Eventually, several factors combined to deny the Cherokees their dream of establishing a viable western nation—mainly continuing hostilities with Osage Indians and pressures emanating from expanding non-Indian settlement in the region.

The 1817 treaty granting Cherokees ownership of lands between the Arkansas and White rivers also stipulated that Cherokees living south of the Arkansas River had to relocate. This forced Duwali, who had settled along the Petit Jean River, to lead his people in 1819 to Lost Prairie, on the west bank of the Red River in southwest Arkansas. The following year Duwali and his followers moved farther west, driven out by a local white "militia" who raided their settlement. By 1822 they were living north of Nacogdoches in

"The Trail of Tears," by Robert Lindneux (courtesy of Woolaroc Museum, Bartlesville, Oklahoma)

eastern Texas. In 1839, at the age of 83, Duwali was killed along the Neches River near Tyler, Texas, while leading his people to battle against the army of the Republic of Texas.

By 1828 the Cherokees remaining in Arkansas had ceded their lands in exchange for lands in northeastern Indian Territory. With their emigration, significant occupation of Arkansas lands by American Indians was brought to an end.

A decade after the Arkansas Cherokees had moved to their new reservation, they were joined by Eastern Cherokees forcibly removed from their homelands in Tennessee, North and South Carolina, Georgia, and Alabama. This long and dolorous journey under the escort of the U.S. army followed routes through northern Arkansas and southern Missouri that came to be known as the Trail of Tears. Factionalism soon developed between the "Old Settlers," who had come from Arkansas, and the "Treaty" and "National" parties representing the eastern immigrants. Violence broke out, and for several years a civil war raged among the opposing Cherokee groups relocated in Indian Territory.

Despite these troubles, many Cherokees became successful farmers. Monies that the Cherokees had received for land cessions were invested and the profits used to pay for the publication of newspapers and to set up a school system. Unlike many other Indian groups, who were forced to rely on the government or on missionaries for the education of their children, the Cherokees organized their own schools and hired native teachers, including Sequoyah. One exception to this self-sufficient educational program was the Dwight Mission, which had relocated to Indian Territory when the Arkansas Cherokees moved in 1828. The new Dwight Mission at Nicksville, along Sallisaw Creek in northeastern Oklahoma had 11 log cabins that housed 65 Cherokee students.

The centerpiece of Cherokee successes in public education was the founding in 1851 of the Cherokee Female Seminary at a time when higher educational opportunities for women were almost unheard of in American society. Unfortunately, costs for supporting the newspapers, schools, and seminary eventually exceeded the income produced by Cherokee investments, forcing the curtailment or termination of many of these programs.

Community festivals and ceremonies remained an important part of Cherokee social life in their Indian Territory settlements. Traditional games and contests were played, and dances and public orations were frequently held. A tribal center was established at Tahlequah in 1839. This center provided a setting not only for Cherokee social and political events, but also for the multitribal or Pan-Indian affairs in which the Cherokees were becoming increasingly involved. For example, in 1843 the Cherokees hosted an Indian council at Tahlequah, at which representatives from 18 tribes gathered to identify common problems and to discuss courses of remedial action.

Although slavery had long been a part of Cherokee culture, by the midnineteenth century many Cherokees—especially traditionalists who sought to remain separate from frontier American society—had come to identify slavery as a repugnant feature of white American culture. This difference of opinion was the root of

Dwight Mission, from a drawing made in 1824 (courtesy of the Arkansas History Commission)

a wide split that opened up among the Cherokees during the Civil War. So intense were the animosities between pro-Union and pro-Confederate Cherokees that they came to carry on their own war against each other in addition to participating in the larger national conflict. When the Civil War finally ended, much negotiation and concessions on both sides were required to reestablish unity among the Cherokee people.

A treaty signed in 1865 between the Cherokees and the United States reasserted Cherokee autonomy on reservation lands but also contained a clause granting rights-of-way to American railroad companies. The railroads brought huge numbers of land-hungry settlers to the western frontier. Intense pressures built up to open Cherokee lands for purchase by non-Indians. Though the Cherokees were steadfast in resisting the allotment of their lands, the federal government went ahead with the allotment program in 1902 and the reservation was brought to an end.

Having lost their land base and their sovereignty, the Western Cherokees dispersed into small communities in northeast Oklahoma after statehood was granted in 1907. Most Cherokees assimilated into white American society, but a few attempted to hold on to cherished traditions. Ceremonial grounds were maintained at several communities, where dances and Green Corn ceremonies continued to be held. One Cherokee leader named Red Bird Smith gathered a number of followers to participate in the Keetoowah Society, a traditional religious organization that provided spiritual refuge for a people who, by the twentieth century, had become culturally disenfranchised and economically disadvantaged.

Throughout most of the twentieth century, the Western Cherokees continued to occupy the impoverished margins of rural American society. Federal programs of the 1960s and 1970s aimed at relieving poverty across the United States provided some assistance for the Cherokees, but no long-term solutions to their problems were developed. Programs to support Indian self-determination projects found limited opportunities among the Oklahoma Cherokees, who remained divided into a minority traditionalist faction and a majority group of assimilated Indians.

In 1975, a new constitution was adopted that provided for the election of tribal officials, who previously were appointed by the Bureau of Indian Affairs. While this did not bring factionalism to an end, tribal elections provided for a more representative form of government. Beginning at about the same time, sustained interests in their cultural heritage led the Western Cherokees to develop an outdoor drama festival at Tahlequah. Since the 1970s, many additional economic, educational, and cultural programs have been developed. Members of the Keetoowah Society are presently attempting to acquire an independent land base.

The Tunicas

Following the Louisiana Purchase in 1803, the U.S. government began to explore, map, and assess the population and settlements of the vast, newly acquired territory. Various other matters soon competed for the attention and resources of the federal government, however, not the least of which were growing concerns about so-called "hostile" Indian tribes on the Western Plains. As a result, many of the smaller Southeastern tribes, including the Tunicas living near Marksville, Louisiana, were left alone throughout most of the nineteenth century. During this period, these Indian groups were able to accommodate themselves gradually to prevailing frontier circumstances.

The Tunica population at the beginning of the nineteenth century was very small—perhaps only about a hundred persons or so. They lived on the fringes of frontier American society, far enough away from white settlements to allow traditional hunting and agricultural practices, yet close enough to these settlements to maintain trade relations through which they could acquire the firearms and other manufactured items, including tools and clothing, that they had come to depend upon. Perhaps because of their well-developed skills as traders, the Tunicas appear to have enjoyed a level of prosperity throughout the nineteenth century above that of many other Southeastern Indians. Their population, at least, did not further decline.

Like many other Southeastern tribes, the Tunicas found they could maintain cultural distinctiveness only on the margins of frontier American society. They could not depend on the federal government for support or assistance in any form, not even justice in legal affairs. Federal policy at this time regarded tribes like the Tunica as mere "savages," who if ignored would eventually disappear.

To maintain their viability, the Tunicas adopted the practice of intermarrying with members of other tribes as well as with blacks and whites. An unforeseen consequence resulted in 1938, when the Bureau of Indian Affairs pronounced that the Tunicas had become "too intermixed to be considered Indians," and the tribe lost its federal recognition. To this loss others were added: in the following decades, the last speakers of the Tunica language died and many traditional ceremonies were discontinued.

Despite these setbacks, the Tunicas continued to fight for restoration of their status as a federally recognized tribe. In 1974 the tribe incorporated itself as the Tunica-Biloxi Indian Tribe of

Louisiana, led by a chairman and Tribal Council. The Tunica-Biloxi tribe won formal recognition by the state of Louisiana in 1975, and in 1981 by the U.S. government. These victories provided the basis for development programs now under way.

5

PERSISTENCE:
Contemporary Perspectives

With the exception of the Koroas, who were assimilated into other tribes in the eighteenth century, all the major Indian groups that once lived in Arkansas survive today. While they participate in many aspects of contemporary American culture, it would be incorrect to say that their own cultures have been lost. It is true that each group has experienced tremendous cultural change since first contact with Europeans, but these changes do not amount to the abandonment of traditional culture. Rather, they represent adjustments made in response to historical circumstances affecting each tribe.

These responses often included the adoption of new beliefs or practices—some developed by the Indians themselves and some borrowed from non-Indians—in ways that preserved major cultural values or themes. The Ghost Dance, peyote religion, powwows, and other revitalization movements are all examples of this process of combining old and new ideas to serve present needs while at the same time preserving connections with cherished tradition. The result for American Indians has been survival into the present of important symbols—reflected not only in dance, song, and art, but also in economic, political, and social arrangements—that are compelling reminders of their singular identity within contemporary American society.

Quapaws with peace medals, left: Bob Whitebird; right: Bill
Supernaw (Arkansas Archeological Survey 85889)

Even more subtle lines of continuity can be identified for Arkansas's native peoples. Historical accounts summarized in previous
chapters portray the Quapaws, for example, as possessing a very
flexible and "open" society, in which organizational changes could be
made, if necessary, to promote independence, autonomy, and self-
determination. This flexibility and openness served the Quapaws
well during the more recent historic era, as they found it necessary to
incorporate various changes in land tenure and political organization
in order to adapt to the American socioeconomic system.

Today, Quapaws have about 2000 members living in many parts
of the United States but mainly in northeast Oklahoma. A tribal
center and powwow grounds are maintained near Miami, Oklahoma.
The tribe is governed by the Business Committee, which oversees an

Quapaws conducting cedar-smoke ceremony at Menard-Hodges site dedication, November 1991 (Arkansas Archeological Survey 916088)

industrial park development and a number of successful businesses and social programs. Annual powwows provide an opportunity for Quapaws to gather with other Indians and with the general public for three days of games and contests, dances, feasts, and socializing.

The Quapaws have always maintained an affinity with their native lands in Arkansas. The Quapaw Business Committee works with the University of Arkansas and with local municipalities on various economic development projects. In 1985 the Quapaws returned to their Arkansas homeland for a symposium sponsored by the Arkansas Endowment for the Humanities (now the Arkansas Humanities Council) and the Southeast Arkansas Science Center. Over 50 members of the tribe joined with scholars and the general public to commemorate Quapaw cultural persistence. In 1991, tribal members again returned to Arkansas to participate in the dedication of the Menard-Hodges site, an archeological site thought to be the location of the seventeenth century village of Osotouy, as a National Historic landmark. This event, as much as any in recent years, underscores the significance of the American Indian past as an important element of our nation's story.

The disposition of prehistoric and historic Indian remains unearthed accidentally or in the context of archeological excavations is an issue that concerns many contemporary Indians. A consecrated burial ground has been established at Toltec Mounds State Park for reburial of Quapaw remains, and the Quapaws have entered into cooperative agreements with the state of Arkansas concerning the disposition of remains which may be unearthed during ongoing archeological research both at Toltec and at Parkin Archeological State Park. In 1991 tribal representatives reburied Quapaw remains unearthed at Eaker Air Force Base near Blytheville. Beginning in 1996, the Quapaws have maintained a relationship with the Arkansas Archeological Survey which provides office support for tribal programs related to the Native American Graves Protection and Repatriation Act.

One of the most noteworthy features of Caddo social organization during the colonial era was their well organized hierarchy of community leaders, whose most important responsibility was to develop alliances to promote the well-being and security of their people. The diplomatic skills developed by these leaders played an important role in the preservation of Caddoan cultural integrity throughout the later historic era.

About 2000 Caddos presently live near Binger and Fort Cobb, Oklahoma. The tribal center at Binger includes government offices, a campground, a community center, and the Caddo Tribal Heritage Museum. The Caddos continue to maintain a distinction between the Hasinai and Kadohadacho linguistic divisions; language preservation programs include classes taught at the University of Oklahoma.

Elected officials manage several programs for young and old and provide a variety of work-training and educational opportunities. Currently there are plans to develop small industries and to encourage independent corporate use of tribal lands in an effort to achieve

Dancers and drummers at the Caddo Conference, Binger, Oklahoma, March 1985

economic self-sufficiency. The Caddos regularly participate in the Caddo Conference, an annual scholarly gathering to discuss current archeological and ethnohistorical research.

Wealth from oil leases has permitted the Osages to remain apart from Pan-Indian associations throughout the twentieth century and exempted them from most federal assistance programs for Indians, which inevitably serve to level out many differences among partici- pant tribes. Thus, the Osages were able to retain a far greater degree of distinctiveness than many of their neighbors.

There are about 10,000 Osages listed on the tribal roll. While most live and work in the larger American society, an autonomous community persists. Though dispersed across a number of towns, mainly in northeastern Oklahoma, members of this community frequently gather for traditional ceremonies, including the iloshka dances, elaborate affairs often involving hundreds of participants. There are three regional iloshka societies, each with its own dance committee, membership group, and dance ground.

The Cherokee Indians are the most numerous of the groups that once lived in Arkansas, numbering approximately 120,000, many of whom reside in northeastern Oklahoma. Government offices, the T'sa'lagi Museum, the Historical Society, and other facilities are maintained at Tahlequah. In 1987 Wilma Mankiller was elected principal chief of the Western Cherokees, thus continuing into the modern era the tradition of leadership by Cherokee women. Successes in various economic developments brought the Western Cherokees assets in excess of $52 million by 1989. Cherokees continue to maintain economic viability in the modern world while at the same time preserving important cultural values.

Today, about 200 members of the Tunica-Biloxi tribe live near Marksville, Louisiana. The Tunica-Biloxi tribe is involved in a concerted effort to become economically self-sufficient. To achieve this status has required the adoption of new economic strategies, including leasing tribal lands to outside business concerns. While such strategies clearly reflect significant cultural changes and the adoption of mainstream American business practices, there is still much evidence of the persistence of old but valued traditions. The maintenance of a tribal government, a distinctive pattern of managing tribal lands that balances individual and community needs, and the continuation of important ceremonies—most notably the annual Corn Feast—all underscore the success of the Tunica-Biloxi in sustaining an identity based on traditional cultural values. With federal funds they have built a tribal administrative building and a museum to house the Tunica Treasure artifacts. They also own and operate a very successful pecan processing plant.

While many residents of Arkansas today claim some American Indian ancestry, most descendants of our state's original inhabitants live in Oklahoma, Louisiana, or other parts of the country. The persistence of their unique cultural identity provides an important connection between the history of our state and the heritage of our nation.

EPILOGUE:
Past, Present, and Future in Contemporary Native American Ritual

On Saturday, 2 November 1991, I had the honor of participating in National Historic Landmark dedication ceremonies at the Menard-Hodges site, a late prehistoric mound center in eastern Arkansas that is also thought to have been the Quapaw village of Osotuoy near which Henri de Tonti established the first Arkansas Post in 1686. About three dozen Quapaws were present for the dedication and a "homecoming" ceremony at the site. Representatives of the National Park Service and The Archaeological Conservancy (which purchased the site, thereby making possible its long-term preservation) were also on hand, along with assorted local residents and a number of archeologists and anthropologists.

The Quapaws performed a cedar smoke ceremony to bless the site and all those gathered in celebration of the homecoming. After prayers were offered to God and Wahkonda, the Quapaw elder conducting the ceremony used a feather fan to cleanse and purify each person with the fragrant cedar smoke. Three leading men of the tribe then carried a kettle containing burning cedar boughs around the large mound.

Later in the day the celebrants gathered at Arkansas Post National Memorial for a formal dedication ceremony, followed by Quapaw dancing, story telling, and craft exhibits. Here I witnessed a very interesting performance late in the afternoon. One of the Quapaw men made a drum by stretching a dressed skin over a small brass kettle partly filled with water. A cord was looped over small pebbles placed beneath the skin around the kettle rim in such a way that the skin could be pulled tight. As the man beat a rhythm on the drum, another elder sang Quapaw songs in the native language while keeping time with an elaborately decorated rattle. Watching this performance, I was reminded of an account written in 1682 by a member of La Salle's expedition when it reached the village of Kappa. The account of describes Quapaws singing songs to the Frenchmen accompanied by "gourds full of pebbles, and. . .drums, which are pots covered with dressed skin."

The following weekend I was sitting in a bus traveling to Pawhuska, Oklahoma, en route to the Osage Tribal Museum and Osage Agency campus. I was listening to a member of the Osage tribe, who holds a Ph.D. degree and who served at the time as executive director of federal program services for the tribe, speaking about Osage culture and history. He mentioned the great importance for contemporary Osages of family and social relations, participation in annual iloshka dances, and various educational programs including native language instruction. All of these were necessary, he emphasized, to keep open and clear the "paths of our children."

The Caddo Conference is an annual meeting of archeologists, anthropologists, historians, and members of the Caddo Nation of Oklahoma who gather to discuss current research and other topics of mutual interest. The conference typically consists of two days of formal presentations and panel discussions followed by a traditional Caddo meal and dance. The meal is always preceded by a performance of the Turkey Dance, which features the women and must be completed before sunset. The first of three dance segments consists of a series of short songs that call the dancers ("Come on, you turkeys!") in several dialects. The second, and by far the longest, segment consists of a series of songs that refer to historical events. Songs about recent events are occasionally added to the repertoire of traditional songs, which consist of accounts stretching back in time to the creation of important features of Caddo landscapes. As these are sung, the head dancer leads the rest of the women in a step that imitates a turkey's gait. In the final segment, the women move out to the surrounding audience to select male partners, who cannot be close relatives and who can only refuse the invitation by offering an article of clothing or a gift of money. In sum, the Turkey Dance celebrates Caddo history and its significance to present circumstances and future prospects.

In these and many other ways, the modern descendants of Arkansas's first inhabitants bring the legacies of their past to bear upon present events so that a positive course can be set for the future.

ANNOTATED BIBLIOGRAPHY

Akridge, Scott
1986 De Soto's Route in North Central Arkansas. *Arkansas Archeological Society Field Notes* 211:3–7. Identifies the location of a salt spring in the lowlands of northeast Arkansas at the province of Calpista according to the Hudson-Morse-Early-Schambach reconstruction of De Soto's route through Arkansas. The De Soto accounts mention an excellent salt springs at Calpista. The site discovered by Akridge is the only salt source known in that part of the state.

Anderson, Melville B. (editor)
1898 *Relation of Henri de Tonty.* The Caxton Club, Chicago. English translation of Henri de Tonti's 1684 memoir of his travels down the Mississippi River with La Salle.

1898 *Relation of the Discovery of the Mississippi River, written from the narrative of Nicolas de La Salle.* Caxton Club, Chicago. English translation of the Nicolas de La Salle account of La Salle's 1682 voyage down the Mississippi River. This account and the one written by Minet (see Weddle, below) provide the most detailed information on the Indians of the Mississippi Valley.

1901 *Relations of the Discoveries and Voyages of Cavelier de La Salle from 1679 to 1681.* Caxton Club, Chicago. Contains an English translation of an anonymous account of discoveries from the Great Lakes region to the mouth of the Mississippi River made by La Salle in 1682.

Arnold, Morris S.

1985 *Unequal Laws unto a Savage Race: European Legal Traditions in Arkansas, 1686–1836.* University of Arkansas Press, Fayetteville. A thoroughly researched study of the French, Spanish, and American legal systems in colonial Arkansas. Examination of the manner in which these legal systems operated in a frontier setting sheds much light on relations between Arkansas Indians and the successive colonial governments under whose legal jurisdiction they lived.

1991 The Myth of John Law's German Colony in Arkansas. In *Arkansas Before the Americans,* edited by Hester A. Davis, pp. 69–73. Arkansas Archeological Survey, Research Series No. 40. Fayetteville. In this short essay Judge Arnold demonstrates that the fabled colony of German settlers along the Arkansas River, supposedly established in 1717 by Scottish financier John Law, really is a fable.

2000 *The Rumble of a Distant Drum: The Quapaws and Old World Newcomers, 1673–1804.* University of Arkansas Press, Fayetteville. A fascinating new study of the interrelationships and cultural accommodations that developed between Quapaws and their French and Spanish neighbors during the colonial era.

Axtell, James

1997 *The Indians' New South: Cultural Change in the Colonial Southeast.* Louisiana State University Press, Baton Rouge. A concise and very useful essay on the impacts of European contact on Southeastern Indians.

Bailey, Garrick

1973 *Changes in Osage Social Organization: 1673–1906.* University of Oregon Anthropological Papers, No. 5. University of Oregon, Eugene. Reconstruction of aboriginal Osage social organization and changes resulting from interaction with Euroamericans.

1995 *Osage and the Invisible World: From the works of Francis La Flesche.* University of Oklahoma Press, Norman. Francis La Flesche (1857–1932), an Omaha Indian and anthropologist employed by the Bureau of American Ethnology, wrote extensively on the Osages and many other Plains Indians. Here Garrick Bailey assembles and provides valuable commentary on some of La Flesche's key works on Osage cosmology and its reflection in ritual.

Baird, W. David

1980 *The Quapaw Indians: A History of the Downstream People.* University of Oklahoma Press, Norman. This book is the standard reference on the history of the Quapaws. It begins with a description of the traditional culture and traces major historical events from the time of first contact with Europeans to the present.

1989 *The Quapaws.* Chelsea House, New York and Philadelphia. A volume in the new "Indians of North America" series by Chelsea House Publishers, this short book traces efforts by the Quapaws to maintain the integrity of their culture through four centuries of interaction with European and American governments and their social and economic institutions. The general reader will find this clearly written and well illustrated book especially appealing.

Bizzell, David W. (editor)

1981 A Report on the Quapaw: The Letters of Governor George Izard to the American Philosophical Society, 1825–1827. *Pulaski County Historical Review* 29:66–79. Contains Paheka's account given to Izard of the Quapaw migration story, plus other ethnographic details concerning the Quapaws.

Bolton, Herbert Eugene

1914 *Athanase de Mèziéres and the Louisiana-Texas Frontier, 1768–1780.* 2 vols. Arthur H. Clark Company, Cleveland. English translations of the correspondence of Athanase de Mèziéres, who served as commandant of the Natchitoches Post under the Spanish colonial government of Louisiana. De Mèziéres played a major role in frontier diplomacy, and his correspondence contains much valuable information on the Caddo Indians and other Southern Plains tribes. An introductory chapter by Bolton summarizes the historical context of de Mèziéres and his activities.

1916 *Spanish Exploration in the Southwest, 1542–1706.* Charles Scribner's Sons, New York. This publication reviews major Spanish expeditions from Mexico into the southwestern United States region and provides English translations of major exploration accounts, including some of the earliest descriptions of Caddo Indians.

1987 *The Hasinais: Southern Caddoans as Seen by the Earliest Europeans.* Edited and with an introduction by Russell M. Magnaghi. University of Oklahoma Press, Norman. Written by Bolton at the beginning of the twentieth century, this book brings together a considerable amount of information drawn from French and Spanish archival sources on one of the major Caddo confederacies. The organization by topical headings (social and political life, economic organization, etc.) makes this a handy reference work.

Bossu, Jean Bernard
1962 *Travels in the Interior of North America, 1751–1762.* Translated and edited by Seymour Feiler. University of Oklahoma Press, Norman. Bossu, a French military officer, traveled widely through the south and visited many Indian communities, including the Quapaws of eastern Arkansas.

Brain, Jeffrey P.
1979 *Tunica Treasure.* Papers of the Peabody Museum of Archaeology and Ethnology, No. 71. Peabody Museum, Harvard University, Cambridge. This is a description and analysis of the famous "Tunica treasure," the burial goods, both aboriginal and European, unearthed from an eighteenth century Tunica site by a grave robber and later returned to the tribe. Brain's study reconstructs processes of cultural change affecting the Tunica, as revealed by the artifacts interred with the dead. This book also provides a valuable overview of Indian-white relations in French colonial Louisiana.

1988 *Tunica Archaeology.* Papers of the Peabody Museum of Archaeology and Ethnology, No. 78. Peabody Museum, Harvard University, Cambridge. This masterful study combines archeological and ethnographic evidence to trace the history, movements, and adaptations of the Tunica people from late prehistoric times to the nineteenth century. Contains extensive technical discussions of archeological manifestations.

1990 *The Tunica-Biloxi.* Chelsea House, New York and Philadelphia. Another volume in the "Indians of North America" series, this book provides a general review of the culture and history of the Tunica-Biloxi people. A valuable basic reference.

Carter, Cecile Elkins
1995 *Caddo Indians: Where We Come From.* University of Oklahoma Press, Norman. An excellent detailed history of the Caddo people written by a member of the Caddo Nation.

Clarke, Mary Whatley
1971 *Chief Bowles and the Texas Cherokees.* University of Oklahoma Press, Norman. A somewhat dated but useful history of the group of Cherokee Indians brought to Arkansas at the turn of the nineteenth century by Chief Bowles (also known as The Bowl and Duwali). In the 1820s, this group moved to Texas.

Clayton, Lawrence A., Vernon James Knight, Jr., and Edward C. Moore (editors)
1993 *The De Soto Chronicles: The Expedition of Hernando de Soto to North America in 1539–1543.* 2 vols. The University of Alabama Press, Tuscaloosa. The De Soto expedition brought the first group of Europeans into direct contact with the native inhabitants of the interior Southeast. These volumes provide new translations of all known accounts of the expedition along with a valuable collection of supplementary essays.

Covey, Cylcone (translator and editor)
1986 *Cabeza de Vaca's Adventures in the Unknown Interior of America.* University of New Mexico Press, Albuquerque. This is an English translation of the adventures of four survivors of the 1528 expedition to southeastern North America of Pánfilo de Narváez. Shipwrecked along the northwest coast of Florida, the survivors trekked overland through Texas and were rescued by Spanish settlers in New Mexico. Provides intriguing glimpses of sixteenth century Indian cultures.

Cox, Isaac Joslin
1922 *The Journeys of René Robert Cavelier, Sieur de La Salle.* 2 vols. Allerton Book Company, New York. These volumes contain English translations of the official report of La Salle's 1682 discovery of the mouth of the Mississippi and Tonti's 1691 memoir of his travels in the Mississippi Valley and surrounding regions.

Crane, Verner
1956 *The Southern Frontier, 1670–1732.* 2nd edition. Duke University Press, Durham. A classic study of colonial settlement in the Southeast, this book discusses English attempts to sway the Quapaws from their alliance with the French during the late seventeenth and early eighteenth centuries.

Crosby, Alfred W.

1973 *The Columbian Exchange: Biological and Cultural Consequences of 1492*. Greenwood Press, Westport, Connecticut. This interesting book discusses the effects of Old World diseases on Native American populations following contact with Europeans.

1986 *Ecological Imperialism: The Biological Expansion of Europe, 900–1900*. Cambridge University Press, Cambridge. An extension of the Columbian exchange idea, Crosby examines the broader ecological consequences of European colonial expansion across the world's temperate climatic zones.

Davis, Hester A.

1987 The Cherokee in Arkansas: An Invisible Archeological Resource. In *Visions and Revisions: Ethnohistoric Perspectives on Southern Cultures*, edited by George Sabo III and William M. Schneider, pp. 48–58. The University of Georgia Press, Athens and London. This article reviews ethnohistoric data on Cherokee settlement in Arkansas to determine where nineteenth century Cherokee sites might be and what archeological patterns might distinguish them from white settlements of the same period.

Davis, Hester A. (editor)

1991 *Arkansas before the Americans*. Arkansas Archeological Survey, Research Series No. 40. Fayetteville. A valuable collection of papers on Arkansas Indians of the colonial era presented at a 1986 conference commemorating the tricentennial of Tonti's founding of Arkansas Post.

Delanglez, Jean

1938 *The Journal of Jean Cavelier: The Account of a Survivor of La Salle's Texas Expedition*. Institute of Jesuit History, Chicago. English translation of Jean Cavelier's journal concerning La Salle's Fort St. Louis settlement on the Texas Gulf Coast, and the trek from that settlement through Caddo Indian territory to Arkansas Post made in 1687 by Cavelier, Henri Joutel, and several others. See also Delanglez's subsequent study entitled "The Authorship of the Journal of Jean Cavelier" in *Mid-America* 25(3): 220–23.

Dickinson, Samuel D.

1980 Historic Tribes in the Ouachita Drainage System of Arkansas. *The Arkansas Archeologist* 21:1–11. A valuable summary of Indians living in southern Arkansas, based on information drawn from diverse archival sources.

1982 *New Travels in North America by Jean-Bernard Bossu 1770–1771.* Northwestern State University of Louisiana Press, Natchitoches, Louisiana. An English translation of Bossu's travel account containing chapters on his visits to Quapaw villages.

1986 The River of Cayas, the Ouachita or the Arkansas River? *Arkansas Archeological Society Field Notes* 209:5–11. A critical review of evidence from Spanish archival sources that questions the accuracy of Hudson's reconstruction of the route of De Soto through Arkansas.

1986 The Quapaw Journey to Red River. *The Pulaski County Historical Review* 34(1):14–23. This article provides a summary of the early nineteenth century removal of the Quapaws from the Arkansas River to the Red River.

1987 Arkansas's Spanish Halberds. *The Arkansas Archeologist* 25 and 26:53–62. Description of four probable sixteenth-century Spanish halberds from Arkansas, identified in the 1930s by Colonel John R. Fordyce, Vice-Chairman of the De Soto Commission appointed by Congress in 1936.

1991 Shamans, Priests, Preachers, and Pilgrims at Arkansas Post. In *Arkansas before the Americans,* edited by Hester A. Davis, pp. 95–104. Arkansas Archeological Survey, Research Series No. 40. Fayetteville. This article identifies and assesses the effects upon the Quapaws of several varieties of Christianity introduced at Arkansas Post from the seventeenth to nineteenth centuries.

Din, Gilbert C. and Abraham P. Nasitir

1983 *The Imperial Osages: Spanish-Indian Diplomacy in the Mississippi Valley.* University of Oklahoma Press, Norman. A detailed examination of eighteenth-century Spanish-Indian relations west of the Mississippi River; provides much valuable information on the Osage Indians and their adaptations to Europeans.

Dunn, William E.

1917 *Spanish and French Rivalry in the Gulf Region of the United States, 1678–1702.* University of Texas Press, Austin. This is an authoritative history of the contest for colonial supremacy between the Spanish and the French in southern North America.

Early, Ann M.

2000 The Caddos of the Trans-Mississippi South. In *Indians of the Greater Southeast: Historical Archaeology and Ethnohistory,* edited by B. G. McEwan, pp. 122–141. University Press of Florida, Gainesville. An up-to-date summary of the prehistoric origins, ethnohistory, and historical archaeology of the Caddo Indians.

Eccles, W. J.

1972 *France in America.* Harper and Row, New York. A short but informative overview on French colonial objectives in North America.

Ehle, John

1988 *Trail of Tears: The Rise and Fall of the Cherokee Nation.* Doubleday, New York. A general history of the Cherokee Indians and their removal in the 1830s from Tennessee, the Carolinas, Georgia, and Alabama to Indian Territory along the route through southern Missouri and northern Arkansas that came to be known as the "Trail of Tears."

Everett, Dianna

1990 *The Texas Cherokees: A People between Two Fires, 1819–1840.* University of Oklahoma Press, Norman and London. A thoroughly researched history of a group of Cherokees brought to Arkansas at the beginning of the nineteenth century by Duwali, otherwise known as The Bowl or Chief Bowles. This study focuses on the departure of this group from Arkansas in the 1820s and their subsequent history in Texas.

Falconer, Thomas

1844 *On the Discovery of the Mississippi.* S. Clark, London. Reprinted 1975, Shoal Creek Publishers, Austin. This book contains an English translation of Tonti's 1684 memoir of La Salle's voyage down the Mississippi River in 1682.

Faye, Stanley

1943 The Arkansas Post of Louisiana: French Domination. *Louisiana Historical Quarterly* 26:633–721. A detailed review of seventeenth and eighteenth century French activities in Arkansas, based on archival sources.

1944 The Arkansas Post of Louisiana: Spanish Domination. *Louisiana Historical Quarterly* 27:629–689. A detailed review of eighteenth-century Spanish activities in Arkansas based on archival sources.

Flores, Dan L. (editor)

1984 *Jefferson & Southwestern Exploration: The Freeman-Custis Accounts of the Red River Expedition of 1806*. University of Oklahoma Press, Norman. Reproduction of the accounts of the Freeman-Custis exploration of the Red River in 1806. The accounts provide valuable information on Caddo Indians and other immigrant tribes along the Red River at the beginning of the American colonial era. Introductory and concluding chapters by Flores provide additional insights.

Folmer, Henry

1953 *Franco-Spanish Rivalry in North America, 1523–1763*. Arthur H. Clark, Glendale, Calif. A general overview of French and Spanish colonial rivalries in the Southeast.

Ford, James A.

1961 Menard Site: The Quapaw Village of Osotuoy on the Arkansas River. *American Museum of Natural History, Anthropological Paper* No. 48:133–191. An archeological report on excavations at the site considered by Ford to be the late seventeenth century Quapaw village of Osotuoy.

Foreman, Grant

1930 *Indians and Pioneers*. University of Oklahoma Press, Norman. A good history of Indian-white relations in the southern frontier, emphasizing the American colonial period.

1932 *Indian Removal: The Emigration of the Five Civilized Tribes of Indians*. University of Oklahoma Press, Norman. A dated but still valuable summary of the nineteenth century removal of eastern Indian tribes to Indian Territory.

1934 *The Five Civilized Tribes: Cherokee, Chickasaw, Choctaw, Creek, Seminole.* University of Oklahoma Press, Norman. This general history includes information on the Cherokees, Chickasaws, and Choctaws in Arkansas.

Galloway, Patricia K. (editor)
1982 *La Salle and His Legacy: Frenchmen and Indians in the Lower Mississippi Valley.* University of Mississippi Press, Jackson. A valuable collection of essays presented at a conference commemorating the 400th anniversary of La Salle's 1682 voyage down the Mississippi River.

1991 Couture, Tonti, and the English-Quapaw Connection: A Revision. In *Arkansas Before the Americans,* edited by Hester A. Davis, pp. 74–94. Arkansas Archeological Survey, Research Series No. 40. Fayetteville. This article examines the activities of Jean Couture, a French trader who worked with the British at the beginning of the eighteenth century, in the context of international competition for control of Indian trade in the Louisiana Territory.

1997 *The Hernando de Soto Expedition: History, Historiography, and "Discovery" in the Southeast.* University of Nebraska Press, Lincoln. This edited volume provides an extensive collection of articles on the authorship and cultural and literary aspects of the De Soto expedition chronicles.

Gibson, Charles
1966 *Spain in America.* Harper Colophon Books, New York. A good overview of Spanish colonial objectives in the New World.

Giraud, Marcel
1974 *A History of French Louisiana.* Vol. I: The Reign of Louis XIV. Translated by Joseph C. Lambert. Louisiana State University Press, Baton Rouge. This is an English translation of the first volume of Giraud's masterful five volume study of French Louisiana. This volume covers the period from 1698 to 1715.

Gregory, Hiram F.
1986 *The Southern Caddo: An Anthology.* Garland, New York and London. A collection of important articles on southern Caddo Indian history and culture.

Griffith, William Joyce

1954 *The Hasinai Indians of East Texas as Seen by Europeans, 1687–1772.* Philological and Documentary Studies Vol. II, No. 3. Middle American Research Institute, Tulane University, New Orleans. An extremely valuable study of Hasinai (Caddo) Indian culture based on information derived from French and Spanish archival sources.

Habig, Marion A.

1934 *The Franciscan Pére Marquette: A Critical Biography of Father Zénobe Membré, O.F.M., La Salle's Chaplain and Missionary Companion 1645(ca.)–1689.* Franciscan Studies 13. Joseph F. Wagner, New York. A biographical history of Father Membré, La Salle's chaplain and traveling companion, which also contains English translations of letters concerning La Salle's 1682 voyage down the Mississippi River written by Membré and Henri de Tonti.

Hodge, Frederick W. (editor)

1907, 1910 *Handbook of Indians North of Mexico.* Bureau of American Ethnology, Bulletin 30, Parts I and II. A dated but still useful source of general information on North American Indians.

Hodge, Frederick W., and Theodore H. Lewis (editors)

1907 *Spanish Explorers in the Southern United States, 1528–1543.* Reprint. Texas A&M University Press, College Station. This book contains English translations of narratives concerning the expeditions of Pánfilo Narváez and Cabeza de Vaca, Coronado, and De Soto.

Hoffman, Michael P.

1977 The Kinkead-Mainard Site, 3PU2, a Late Prehistoric Quapaw Phase Site near Little Rock, Arkansas. *The Arkansas Archeologist* 16, 17, and 18:1–41. A technical analysis of an archeological collection from a late prehistoric site in the central Arkansas Valley. Originally identified as an example of a late sixteenth-century Quapaw site, Hoffman now believes the site may have been occupied by prehistoric Tunicans. See Hoffman, 1986, 1990.

1986 Protohistory of the Lower and Central Arkansas River Valley in Arkansas. In *The Protohistoric Period in the Mid-South: 1500–1700.* Proceedings of the 1983 Mid-South Archaeological Conference, edited by

David H. Dye and Ronald C. Brister, pp. 24–37. Archaeological Report No. 18. Mississippi Department of Archives and History, Jackson. This article summarizes present evidence on late prehistoric to early historic period cultural developments in eastern Arkansas.

1990 The Terminal Mississippian Period in the Arkansas River Valley and Quapaw Ethnogenesis. In *Towns and Temples along the Mississippi,* edited by David H. Dye and Cheryl Anne Cox, pp. 202–226. The University of Alabama Press, Tuscaloosa. A summary of archeological and ethnohistoric evidence in support of the hypothesis that the Quapaws migrated to Arkansas following the departure of De Soto's army in 1543.

1991 Quapaw Structures, 1673–1834, and Their Comparative Significance. In *Arkansas before the Americans,* edited by Hester A. Davis, pp. 55–68. Arkansas Archeological Survey, Research Series No. 40. This article draws together ethnohistoric accounts of Quapaw house architecture in support of the Quapaw migration hypothesis.

1993 The Depopulation and Abandonment of Northeastern Arkansas in the Protohistoric Period. In *Archaeology of Eastern North America: Papers in Honor of Stephen Williams,* edited by James B. Stoltman, pp. 261–275. Archaeological Report No. 25. Mississippi Department of Archives and History, Jackson. A summary of bioarcheological perspectives on the protohistoric era in northeastern Arkansas.

1994 Ethnic Identities and Cultural Change in the Protohistoric Period of Eastern Arkansas. In *Perspectives on the Southeast,* edited by Patricia B. Kwachka, pp. 61–70. Southern Anthropological Society Proceedings No. 27. The University of Georgia Press. Athens and London. A valuable update of views expressed in Hoffman's earlier articles on the protohistoric era in eastern Arkansas.

Hoffman, Paul
1991 *A New Andalucia and a Way to the Orient: The American Southeast during the Sixteenth Century.* Louisiana State University Press, Baton Rouge. This book provides an authoritative review of early Spanish exploration in southeastern North America, from the voyage of Juan Ponce de León to the exploration of Hernando de Soto.

House, John H.

1991 The Mississippian Sequence in the Menard Locality, Eastern Arkansas. In *Arkansas before the Americans,* edited by Hester A. Davis, pp. 6–39. Arkansas Archeological Survey Research Series No. 40. This is a descriptive summary of the late prehistoric ceramic sequence for the Menard locality near the confluence of the Arkansas and Mississippi rivers. Bears importantly on the question of Quapaw cultural origins since it was in this area that the Quapaws were first encountered by French explorers in the late seventeenth century.

Hudson, Charles

1976 *The Southeastern Indians.* University of Tennessee Press, Knoxville. The standard reference on the cultures of American Indian tribes in southeastern North America.

1985 De Soto in Arkansas: A Brief Synopsis. *Arkansas Archeological Society Field Notes* 205:3–12. This article details Hudson's first reconstruction of the route of De Soto through Arkansas. According to this reconstruction, the Spaniards spent nearly two years during 1541–1543 wandering through the state.

1990 *The Juan Pardo Expeditions.* Smithsonian Institution Press, Washington, D.C. This is a detailed study of original documents concerning the 1566–1568 explorations of Juan Pardo through the Carolinas and Tennessee. Because Pardo retraced some of De Soto's route through this portion of the Southeast, this study has important bearing on debates concerning the route of De Soto. There is also much information to be found in this book concerning sixteenth-century Southeastern Indians and their contacts with Spanish explorers.

1997 *Knights of Spain, Warriors of the Sun: Hernando de Soto and the South's Ancient Chiefdoms.* University of Georgia Press, Athens. A fascinating and detailed reconstruction of the epic journey of Hernando de Soto across the Southeast and Spanish encounters with the native inhabitants of that vast region.

Jeter, Marvin D.

1986 Tunicans West of the Mississippi: A Summary of Early Historic and Archaeological Evidence. In *The Protohistoric Period in the Mid-South: 1500–1700.* Proceedings of the 1983 Mid-South Archaeological

Conference, edited by David H. Dye and Ronald C. Brister, pp. 38–63. Archaeological Report No. 18. Mississippi Department of Archives and History, Jackson. This article reviews archeological and ethnohistoric evidence of late prehistoric and early historic Tunica Indians in eastern Arkansas.

Jeter, Marvin D., Jerome C. Rose, G. Ishmael Williams, Jr., and Anna M. Harmon
1989 *Archeology and Bioarcheology of the Lower Mississippi Valley and Trans-Mississippi South in Arkansas and Louisiana.* Arkansas Archeological Survey Research Series No. 37. Fayetteville. This is a technical cultural resource overview that contains useful discussions of protohistoric and historic Native Americans.

John, Elizabeth A. H.
1975 *Storms Brewed in Other Men's Worlds: The Confrontation of Indians, Spanish, and French in the Southwest, 1540–1795.* University of Nebraska Press, Lincoln and London. A long book but well worth reading for the extensive and in depth treatment of Indian-white relations in the vast region stretching from New Mexico to Louisiana, in which Franco-Spanish struggles for colonial supremacy were carried on for nearly two and a half centuries.

Joutel, Henri
1962 *Joutel's Journal of La Salle's Last Voyage.* Edited and with an introduction by Henry Reed Stiles. Reprint. Corinth, New York. This is a facsimile edition of a highly abridged English translation of Joutel's journal published in England in 1714. The original manuscript no longer exists, but a French version of the longer journal is printed in Pierre Margry's Découvertes etáblissements des français dans l'ouest et dans le sud de l'Amérique septentrionale (1614–1754). 6 vols. Maisonneuve, Paris (1876–86).

Kellogg, Louise Phelps
1917 *Early Narratives of the Northwest, 1634–1699.* Charles Scribner's Sons, New York. Contains English translations of reports and journals concerning voyages down the Mississippi River by Marquette and Jolliet, La Salle, and Henri de Tonti.

Kidder, Tristam R.
1988 The Koroa Indians of the Lower Mississippi Valley. *Mississippi Ar-*

chaeology 23(2):1–42. This useful article summarizes archeological and ethnohistoric evidence of Koroa Indians (a Tunica-speaking tribe) in southeast Arkansas and northern Louisiana.

King, Duane H.
1979 *The Cherokee Indian Nation: A Troubled History.* The University of Tennessee Press, Knoxville. A valuable collection of essays, mainly on the Eastern Cherokees.

Kinnaird, Lawrence
1945 *Spain in the Mississippi Valley, 1765–1794.* 3 vols. Annual Report of the American Historical Association for 1945, Washington, D.C. This volume contains English translations of official Spanish correspondence concerning the Mississippi Valley, some of which contains information on relations with Indians.

Kniffen, Fred D., Hiram F. Gregory, and George A. Stokes
1987 *The Historic Indian Tribes of Louisiana.* Louisiana State University Press, Baton Rouge. A valuable reference on the Indian tribes of Louisiana. Chapters review major prehistoric and historic developments as well as specific topics (languages, arts and crafts, etc.).

LaVere, David
1998 *The Caddo Chiefdoms: Caddo Economics and Politics, 700–1835.* University of Nebraska Press, Lincoln. This book examines how the Caddos used traditional economic, political, religious, and social institutions to create relationships with Euroamerican colonists, and the cultural changes these relationships produced.

La Flesche, Francis
1924 *Ethnology of the Osage Indian.* Miscellaneous Collection, No. 76. Smithsonian Institution, Washington, D.C. This is an encyclopedic study of traditional Osage culture written by a Bureau of American Ethnology anthropologist who was also a member of the Omaha tribe.

La Harpe, Jean-Baptiste Benard de
1971 *The Historical Journal of the Establishment of the French in Louisiana.* Translated by Joan Cain and Virginia Koenig, edited and annotated by Glenn R. Conrad. Center for Louisiana Studies, University of Southwestern Louisiana, Lafayette. This is a lengthy historical account of French activities in colonial Louisiana (which includes Arkansas),

emphasizing La Harpe's experiences in the colony from 1719 to 1722. It appears to have been written by La Harpe between 1723 and 1726, when he was in France.

Le Page du Pratz, Antoine Simon
1974 *The History of Louisiana*. Edited by Joseph G. Tregle, Jr. Louisiana State University Press, Baton Rouge. A highly abridged English translation of Le Page du Pratz's 1758 Histoire de la Louisiane, this volume provides interesting details on eighteenth century Indian life.

McDermott, John F. (editor)
1940 *Tixier's Travels on the Osage Prairies*. Translated by Albert J. Salavan. University of Oklahoma Press, Norman. This is Victor Tixier's first hand account of traditional Osage culture, written in the mid-eighteenth century.

1969 *Frenchmen and French Ways in the Mississippi Valley*. University of Illinois Press, Urbana. This collection of essays by various scholars provides a good overview of colonial French activities in the Mississippi Valley.

1974 *The Spanish in the Mississippi Valley, 1762–1804*. University of Illinois Press, Urbana. More scholarly essays on Spanish colonial affairs in the Mississippi Valley.

McEwan, Bonnie G.
2000 *Indians of the Greater Southeast: Historical Archaeology and Ethnohistory*. University Presses of Florida, Gainesville. A valuable collection of essays summarizing recent research and our current state of knowledge about Southeastern Indians, including selections on the Caddos, Chickasaws, Cherokees, and Quapaws.

Markman, Robert P.
1972 *The Arkansas Cherokees: 1817–1828*. Ph.D. dissertation, University of Oklahoma. University Microprints, Ann Arbor. The only in-depth historical study of Arkansas Cherokees. Unfortunately, this valuable work is an unpublished doctoral dissertation that is available in only a few libraries in the state.

Mathews, John Joseph
1932 *Wah'Kon-tah: The Osage and the White Man's Road*. University of Oklahoma Press, Norman. Mathews, an Osage Indian, writes on the

history of his people and their adaptations to nineteenth and twentieth century events.

1961 *The Osages: Children of the Middle Waters.* University of Oklahoma Press, Norman. This is a comprehensive history and ethnography of the Osage written by a prominent member of the tribe.

Milanich, Jerald T., and Susan Milbrath (editors)
1989 *First Encounters: Spanish Explorations in the Caribbean and the United States, 1492–1570.* Ripley P. Bullen Monographs in Anthropology and History, No. 9. Florida Museum of Natural History and University of Florida Press, Gainesville. This lavishly illustrated book contains a valuable collection of essays by many scholars that touch on a number of subjects ranging from the world view of fifteenth century Europeans to various Spanish attempts to explore and colonize the New World. There is an article by Charles Hudson and his colleagues on De Soto's expedition through southeastern North America.

Miller, Jay
1996 Changing Moons: A History of Caddo Religion. *Plains Anthropologist* 41:243–259. A study of the history of religion among the Caddos, linking historic and modern developments to ancient concepts.

Morse, Dan F. (editor)
1989 *Nodena: An Account of 90 Years of Archeological Investigation in Southeast Mississippi County, Arkansas.* Arkansas Archeological Survey, Research Series No. 30. Fayetteville. This volume contains articles by specialists summarizing the archeology and bioanthropology of the Nodena phase, a late prehistoric and protohistoric cultural manifestation in northeast Arkansas that Morse believes is ancestral to historic Quapaw culture.

Morse, Dan F.
1990 The Nodena Phase. In *Towns and Temples along the Mississippi,* edited by David H. Dye and Cheryl Anne Cox, pp. 69–97. The University of Alabama Press, Tuscaloosa. This article provides a summary of an archeological phase that Morse believes is ancestral to historic Quapaw Indians.

1991 On the Possible Origin of the Quapaws in Northeast Arkansas. In *Arkansas before the Americans,* edited by Hester A. Davis, pp. 40–54. Arkansas Archeological Survey, Research Series No. 40. Fayetteville. This article summarizes archeological and historical evidence in support of the hypothesis that historic Quapaw culture developed from late prehistoric and protohistoric antecedents in northeast Arkansas.

Morse, Dan F., and Phyllis A. Morse
1983 *Archaeology of the Central Mississippi Valley.* Academic Press, New York. This is the standard reference on the archeology of eastern Arkansas and adjacent regions. Chapters treating the late prehistoric to historic periods summarize the Morses' views on the De Soto expedition and the origin of the Quapaw Indians.

1990 The Spanish Exploration of Arkansas. In *Columbian Consequences, Vol. 2: Archaeological and Historical Perspectives on the Spanish Borderlands East,* edited by David Hurst Thomas, pp. 197–210. Smithsonian Institution Press, Washington, D.C. A short article summarizing the Hudson-Morse-Early-Schambach reconstruction of De Soto's route through Arkansas and the Indian societies the Spaniards encountered.

Morse, Phyllis A.
1981 *Parkin: The 1978–1979 Archeological Investigations of a Cross County Site.* Arkansas Archeological Survey, Research Series No. 13. Fayetteville. This report summarizes archeological research at the Parkin site in Cross County, thought to be the location of the village of Casqui visited by De Soto in 1541.

1990 The Parkin Site and the Parkin Phase. In *Towns and Temples along the Mississippi,* edited by David H. Dye and Cheryl Anne Cox, pp. 118–134. The University of Alabama Press, Tuscaloosa. This is an updated summary of the Parkin site, thought to be the village of Casqui visited by De Soto, and the Parkin phase, a late prehistoric archeological manifestation in northeast Arkansas considered by Dan and Phyllis Morse to be ancestral to the Quapaw Indians.

Murphy, Edmund R.
1941 *Henry de Tonty: Fur Trader on the Mississippi.* Johns Hopkins Press, Baltimore. A thorough biographical history of Henri de Tonti and his exploits in the Mississippi Valley.

Newcomb, W. W.

1961 *The Indians of Texas.* University of Texas Press, Austin and London. A good overview of the culture and history of the Indians of Texas; contains chapters on Plains Caddoans and southern Caddoans.

Newkumet, Vynola Beaver, and Howard L. Meredith

1988 *Hasinai: A Traditional History of the Caddo Confederacy.* Texas A&M University Press, College Station. A valuable description of contemporary cultural traditions among the Hasinais. The late Vynola Beaver Newkumet was a member of the Hasinais.

Nuttall, Thomas

1980 *A Journal of Travels into the Arkansas Territory during the Year 1819.* University of Oklahoma Press, Norman. Nuttall's early nineteenth century travels in eastern Arkansas and up the Arkansas River brought him into contact with Quapaw and Cherokee Indians, whose villages and customs he describes.

Perdue, Theda

1979 *Slavery and the Evolution of Cherokee Society, 1540–1866.* University of Tennessee Press, Knoxville. This is a detailed examination of the role of slavery in Cherokee society, the internal tensions it created, and its influence on Cherokee responses to Euroamericans.

1989 *The Cherokee.* Chelsea House Publishers, New York and Philadelphia. Another volume in the "Indians of North America" series, this is a short but valuable summary of Cherokee cultural history. While most emphasis is on the Eastern Cherokee, some information on the Western Cherokee is provided.

Phillips, Philip, James A. Ford, and James B. Griffin

1951 *Archaeological Survey in the Lower Mississippi Alluvial Valley, 1940–47.* Papers of the Peabody Museum of Archaeology and Ethnology, No. 25. Peabody Museum, Harvard University, Cambridge. A portion of this report deals with the De Soto route. There are also discussions on connections between archeological complexes and historic Indian tribes in the Mississippi Valley. The authors challenge the 1939 De Soto Commission route in Arkansas, based on their own surveys.

Quinn, David B.

1979 *New American World: A Documentary History of North America to 1612*. 5 vols. Arno Press, New York. These volumes contain English translations of European exploration accounts, including those relating to the De Soto expedition.

Rollings, Willard H.

1992 *The Osage: An Ethnohistorical Study of Hegemony on the Prairie-Plains*. University of Missouri Press, Columbia. This book provides a detailed examination of the historical role played by the Osages as "middlemen" in the fur trade connecting Plains tribes with European trading posts in the Mississippi Valley.

Rowland, Dunbar, and A. G. Sanders (editors)

1927–32 *Mississippi Provincial Archives: The French Dominion, 1704–1743*. 3 vols. Press of the Mississippi Department of Archives and History, Jackson. Voluminous compilation of translated primary accounts, mostly official correspondence, many of which contain valuable information about Indians.

Rowland, Dunbar, A. G. Sanders, and Patricia Kay Galloway (editors)

1984 *Mississippi Provincial Archives: French Dominion, 1729–1763*. 2 vols. Louisiana State University Press, Baton Rouge. More translations of primary accounts.

Sabo, George III

1987 Reordering Their World: A Caddoan Ethnohistory. In *Visions and Revisions: Ethnohistoric Perspectives on Southern Cultures*, edited by George Sabo III and William M. Schneider, pp. 25–47. The University of Georgia Press, Athens and London. A study of changes in Caddo social organization resulting from interaction with Europeans.

1991 Inconsistent Kin: French-Quapaw Relations at Arkansas Post. In *Arkansas before the Americans*, edited by Hester A. Davis, pp. 105–130. Arkansas Archeological Survey, Research Series No. 40. Fayetteville. This article examines the role of native ritual in seventeenth and eighteenth century relations between Quapaws and Europeans.

1995 Rituals of Encounter: Interpreting Native American Views of European Explorers. In *Cultural Encounters in Early America: Native Americans and Europeans in Arkansas*, edited by Jeannie M. Whayne, pp. 76–87. University of Arkansas Press, Fayetteville. A comparison of Caddo and Quapaw uses of the calumet ceremony to receive and welcome European explorers in the late eighteenth century.

1996 The Quapaws. In *The Encyclopedia of the American Indian*, edited by Frederick E. Hoxie. Houghton Mifflin, New York. A brief overview of Quapaw culture. The volume contains hundreds of other useful articles.

1998 The Structure of Caddo Leadership in the Colonial Era. In *The Native History of the Caddo: Their Place in Southeastern Archeology and Ethnohistory*, edited by Timothy K. Perttula and James E. Bruseth, pp. 159–174. Studies in Archeology 30. Texas Archeological Research Laboratory, The University of Texas, Austin. An examination of the persistence of Caddo institutions of leadership in the early historic era.

2000 The Quapaw Indians of Arkansas, 1673–1803. In *Indians of the Greater Southeast: Historical Archaeology and Ethnohistory*, edited by B. G. McEwen, pp. 178–202. University Press of Florida, Gainesville. A study of cultural interactions between the Quapaws and their French and Spanish neighbors in colonial Arkansas.

Sabo, George III, Ann M. Early, Jerome C. Rose, Barbara A. Burnett, Louis Vogele, Jr., and James P. Harcourt
1988 *Human Adaptations in the Ozark and Ouachita Mountains.* Arkansas Archeological Survey, Research Series No. 31. Fayetteville. A technical cultural resource overview that contains discussions of protohistoric and historic Native Americans in the mountainous regions of western Arkansas.

Sauer, Carl O.
1971 *Sixteenth-Century North America: The Land and the Peoples as Seen by the Europeans.* University of California Press, Berkeley. A scholarly but highly readable study of early explorations in North America, including those of Coronado and De Soto.

Schambach, Frank F.
1989 The End of the Trail: The Route of Hernando de Soto's Army through Southwest Arkansas and East Texas. *The Arkansas Archeologist* 27 and 28:9–33. Schambach compares archeological evidence of sixteenth century Caddo population distributions with the De Soto

narratives and offers a new reconstruction of the route followed by the Spaniards through southwest Arkansas and eastern Texas.

Shea, John Gilmary (editor)
1861 *Early Voyages Up and Down the Mississippi.* Joel Munsell, New York. This book contains English translations of letters from Jesuit missionaries who described many Mississippi Valley tribes, including Quapaws, Koroas, and Tunicas.

Smith, Buckingham
1968 *Narratives of De Soto in the Conquest of Florida.* Palmetto Books, Gainesville. This volume contains English translations of the Biedma and Elvas accounts, various other documents concerning De Soto's expedition, and a chapter on the life of De Soto.

Smith, Ralph A.
1951 Exploration of the Arkansas River, by Benard de La Harpe [sic]. *Arkansas Historical Quarterly* 10(4):339–63. This is an English translation of extracts from the version of La Harpe's journal of his 1722 Arkansas River exploration published by Pierre Margry. It reproduces Margry's transcription errors.

Smith, F. T.
1995 *The Caddo Indians: Tribes at the Convergence of Empires, 1542–1854.* Texas A&M University Press, College Station. This book provides a well-written history of the Caddo Indians from their first encounters with the Hernando de Soto expedition to their removal to the Brazos Reserve in Texas.

1996 *The Caddos, the Wichitas, and the United States, 1846-1901.* Texas A&M University Press, College Station. Picking up where the previous volume left off, this book traces the history of the Caddo Indians during the American era.

Story, Dee Ann
1978 Some Comments on Anthropological Studies Concerning the Caddo. In *Texas Archeology, Essays Honoring R. King Harris,* edited by Kurt D. House, pp. 46–68. Institute for the Study of Earth and Man, Reports of Investigations, No. 3. Southern Methodist Press, Dallas. This essay provides a brief but incisive review of cultural, archeological, linguistic, and bioanthropological studies of the Caddo.

Story, Dee Ann, Janice A. Guy, Barbara A. Burnett, Martha Doty Free-
    man, Jerome C. Rose, D. Gentry Steele, Ben W. Olive, and Karl J.
    Reinhard
1990 *The Archeology and Bioarcheology of the Gulf Coastal Plain*. 2 vols.
    Arkansas Archeological Survey, Research Series No. 38. Fayetteville. A
    detailed cultural resource overview that contains discussions of proto-
    historic and historic Native Americans in southern Texas, including the
    Caddo.

Swan, Daniel C.
1998 Early Osage Peyotism. *Plains Anthropologist* 43:51–71. A brief his-
    tory of Osage participation in the Native American Church.

1999 *Peyote Religious Art: Symbols of Faith and Belief*. University Press
    of Mississippi, Jackson. Written to accompany an exhibition at the
    Gilcrease Museum in Tulsa, Oklahoma, this well-illustrated volume
    provides an excellent overview of the peyote religion and the Native
    American Church among the native tribes of the Trans-Mississippi
    South.

Swanton, John R.
1942 *Source Material on the History and Ethnology of the Caddo Indians*.
    Bureau of American Ethnology, Bulletin 132. Government Printing
    Office, Washington, D.C. This is the standard source for ethnographic
    information on the Caddo Indians, drawn mainly from archival sources.

1979 *The Indians of the Southeastern United States*. Classics in Smithsonian
    Anthropology. Smithsonian Institution Press, Washington, D.C. An
    encyclopedic compilation of ethnographic information on Southeastern
    Indians, much of it derived from archival sources.

1985 *Final Report of the United States De Soto Expedition Commission*. Intro-
    duction by Jeffrey P. Brain and Foreword by William C. Sturtevant.
    Classics of Smithsonian Anthropology. Smithsonian Institution Press,
    Washington, D.C. This book contains the summary of historical, geo-
    graphical, and archeological evidence available in the 1930s concerning
    De Soto's expedition, and the route of travel reconstructed by the Com-
    mission on the basis of that evidence. This reprinting of the original
    report contains a valuable introductory essay by Brain.

Tanner, Helen Hornbeck
1974 *Caddoan Indians IV.* Garland, New York and London. This is a thorough compilation of historical information on nineteenth century Caddo settlements in Oklahoma, and a summary of events leading up to their removal from Texas, Louisiana, and Arkansas.

Thompson, Laura H.
1982 *Historical Translation of Antoine Barraque Manuscript.* M.A. thesis, University of Arkansas, Fayetteville. This is an English translation of the diary kept by Indian agent Antoine Barraque as he led the Quapaw Indians to their Red River settlement in 1826.

Thornton, Russell
1990 *The Cherokees: A Population History.* University of Nebraska Press, Lincoln. This volume examines the historical impacts on Cherokee demography of warfare, disease, removal, and American government efforts to eradicate Native American traditions.

Usner, Daniel H., Jr.
1992 *Indians, Settlers, & Slaves in a Frontier Exchange Economy: The Lower Mississippi Valley before 1783.* University of North Carolina Press, Chapel Hill. This important volume examines the development of economic and cultural interactions among Indians, Europeans, and African slaves in colonial Louisiana.

1998 *American Indians in the Lower Mississippi Valley: Social and Economic Histories.* University of Nebraska Press, Lincoln. A useful collection of essays on Native American and European interactions, including essays on population history, the frontier exchange economy, the early cotton economy, and nineteenth century images of Mississippi Valley Indians.

Weddle, Robert S. (editor)
1987 *La Salle, the Mississippi, and the Gulf: Three Primary Documents.* Texas A&M University Press, College Station. This book contains English translations of Minet's journal of La Salle's 1682 voyage down the Mississippi River and the 1684 voyage to the Texas Gulf Coast; Enriquez Barroto's diary of the 1684 voyage; the interrogation of the Talon brothers, survivors of La Salle's Texas Gulf Coast settlement who spent many years living among Caddo Indians; and valuable critical essays by a number of scholars.

Whayne, Jeannie (compiler)

1995 *Cultural Encounters in the Early South: Indians and Europeans in Arkansas.* University of Arkansas Press, Fayetteville. This volume provides an interesting collection of essays on various aspects of European interaction with the native inhabitants of Arkansas in the colonial era.

Wilson, Terry P.

1985 *The Underground Reservation: Osage Oil.* University of Nebraska Press, Lincoln. This is a detailed study of the turn-of-the-century discovery of oil on Osage lands and its effects on the Osage people.

1988 *The Osage.* Chelsea House, New York and Philadelphia. A volume in the "Indians of North America" series, this is perhaps the most accessible summary of the history and culture of the Osage Indians.

Woodward, Grace Steele

1963 *The Cherokees.* University of Oklahoma Press, Norman. This book is a somewhat dated general history of the Cherokee Indians.

Wright, J. Leitch

1981 *The Only Land They Knew: The Tragic Story of the American Indians in the Old South.* The Free Press, New York. This is a good review of Southeastern Indians, from early historic times to the present.

Young, Gloria A., and Michael P. Hoffman (editors)

1993 *The Expedition of Hernando de Soto West of the Mississippi, 1541–1543.* University of Arkansas Press, Fayetteville. This volume, from a symposium series held at the University of Arkansas in 1988 and 1990, contains a valuable collection of articles that examine a variety of topics concerning the De Soto expedition following the crossing of the Mississippi River in 1541.

Index